my fitness journal

Name _____

Date _____

my fitness journal

RYLAND
PETERS
& SMALL
LONDON NEW YORK

Sam Murphy

with photography by
Chris Everard

CONTENTS

MY BODY	7
MY EXERCISE PROGRAM	17
THE BASICS	31
MY NUTRITION	41
STAYING MOTIVATED	49
MY JOURNAL	55

INTRODUCTION

Congratulations on deciding to keep a fitness journal. You'll soon wonder how you managed without one. This journal will help you choose the right exercise for you, identify your strengths and weaknesses, and keep track of your workouts—as well as improving motivation by showing you just how far you've come.

Nothing worth having in life comes easy, and fitness is no exception; but the rewards that you will reap for just a little effort will make it well worthwhile. So where do you start?

It is no good having a vague idea that you want to "get fit." You need to decide exactly what you are going to do, when, why, and how. That is why the first two sections of the journal, My Body and My Exercise Program, are devoted to precisely those issues—showing you the benefits of regular exercise and how to get the balance right, with a wealth of advice on training. The Basics deals with posture, warming up and cooling down, and stretching.

Eating and drinking the right things are also important in maintaining a healthy body weight and in optimizing the benefits of exercise, as explained in My Nutrition—and completing the nutrition checklist every six weeks will reveal how well you are putting healthy eating into practice. Staying Motivated is full of hints and tips, including ways to integrate exercise into your busy life and make workouts more productive.

Progress is a great motivator. Filling in the weekly exercise log, My Journal—arranged in six training periods of six weeks each—enables you to monitor how far you have come, while completing the Taking Stock page every six weeks allows you to assess whether you are still on track, and to make any necessary adjustments to your program.

Fill in as much detail as possible in the journal pages about your workouts. Even if you encounter a bad patch, when your exercise regime falls by the wayside for a few days (or even longer), keep note of anything that you do manage to achieve—that way, you won't feel as if you have gone back to square one, and you will also have a clearer picture of where and why things went wrong.

Whether you are a workout veteran or this is the first time you have embarked on an exercise regime, you will soon discover that recording your goals, aspirations, observations, and achievements is enlightening and inspirational—and provides hours of entertaining reading. This is your fitness journal. Enjoy it!

MY FITNESS NUMBERS

MY HEALTH CLUB/GYM
_____

MY PERSONAL TRAINER
_____

MY PHYSIOTHERAPIST/
SPORTS INJURY CLINIC
_____

MY SPORTS MASSAGE
THERAPIST
_____

MY FAVORITE SPORT AND
FITNESS WEBSITES
_____
_____
_____
_____

OTHER USEFUL NUMBERS
_____
_____
_____
_____
_____

THE BENEFITS OF EXERCISE

Our bodies were designed to move. They yearn for movement—to stretch, run, leap, dance, curl, and twist. Yet most of us leave behind such activities with our school days. Adults in the developed world burn 500 calories per day less through physical activity than our predecessors did 50 years ago. Thanks to labor-saving gadgets, a constant battle against the clock, and increasingly insular, indoor habits (associated with TV and computers, for example), we have become more sedentary, less healthy, more stressed—and more overweight.

Inactivity is bad for health. It can cause postural problems, backache, and neck tension. If we don't exercise, we lack energy and muscle tone, and even mild exertion leaves us breathless. And—while a slower metabolism, muscle loss, an increase in body fat, and reduced mobility used to be seen simply as part of "aging"—experts now believe that it's the decline in activity that accompanies aging, rather than aging itself, that's to blame.

You may see yourself as very active, but consider whether you are really using your body or whether you are simply busy—rushing around but usually in the car, in the elevator, on the phone. If your physical activity is limited, it is not too late to reverse the trend. Even people in their 70s and 80s who embark on exercise regimes can see satisfying results. Research has shown that active women aged 55–64 gain less than a quarter of the body fat gained by inactive women, while healthy men and women aged 60–70 who run for 45 minutes on four days a week can increase their aerobic fitness by 24 percent in under a year.

Expending a minimum of 1,000 calories a week in physical activity will make you healthier and fitter. It will also enable you to achieve and maintain a body weight that you are happy with, because, when it comes to weight maintenance, energy in = energy out. In other words, if you consume more calories than you burn, you gain weight. Using both diet and exercise to assist you in losing weight works better than diet or exercise alone. Diet is covered in My Nutrition (pages 41–48), but this chapter focuses on the benefits of regular exercise.

> "Mens sana in corpore sano."
> ("A sound mind in a sound body.")
> JUVENAL AD60–130.

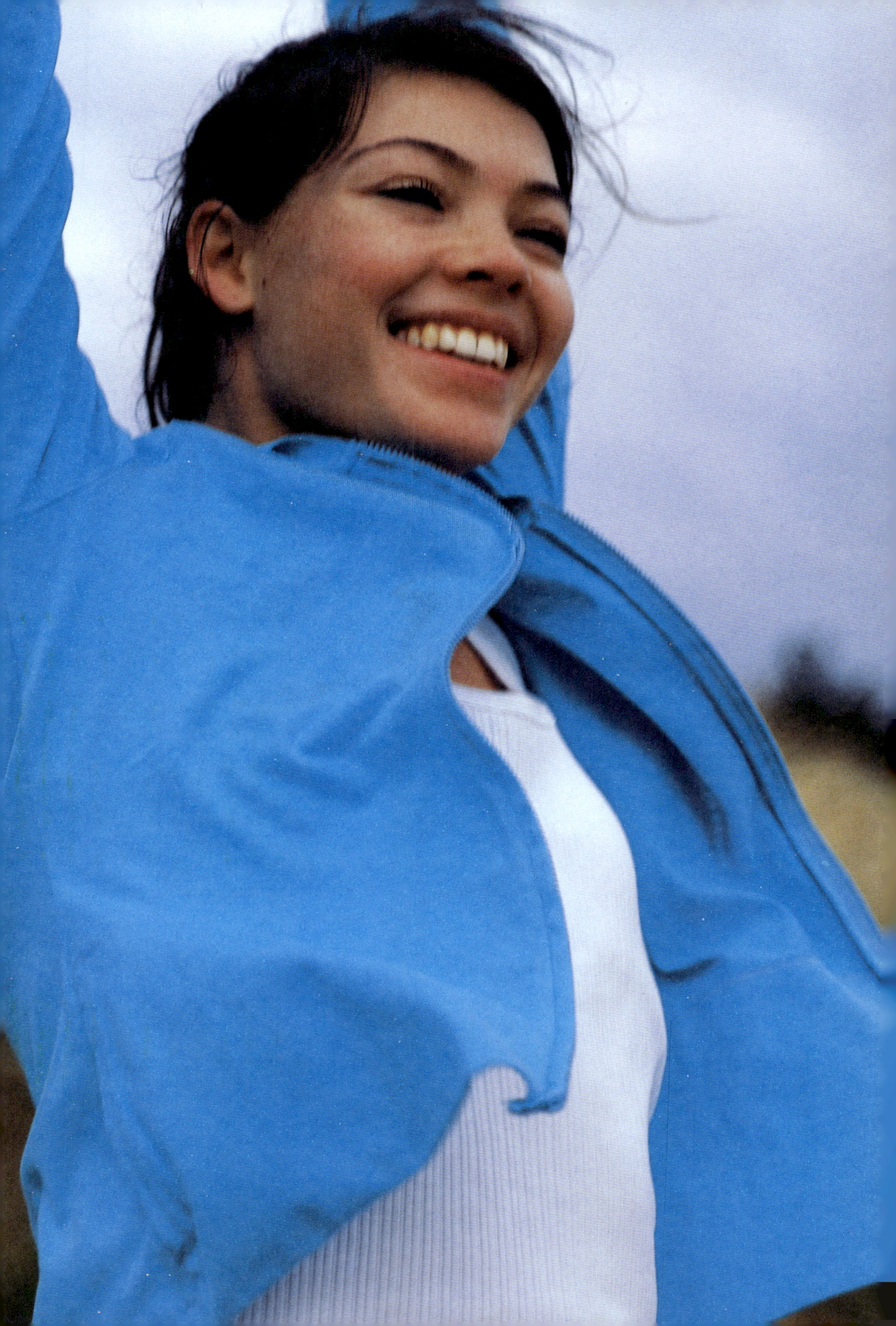

TEN WAYS IN WHICH REGULAR EXERCISE IMPROVES YOUR LIFE

1 Exercise reduces the risk of heart disease and cardiovascular disease
One large-scale study found that very active people were 46 percent less likely to die of cardiovascular disease than sedentary people. Lung capacity and the efficiency of the lungs in extracting oxygen from inhaled air improve with regular aerobic exercise.

2 It improves stress resilience
A recent research study at the University of Georgia found that, in response to stressful situations, the fittest women had less dramatic increases in blood pressure than less fit women.

3 It preserves bone density
Regular impact exercise (in which your weight is not supported) helps keep bones strong and protects against the risk of fractures and frailty due to osteoporosis in later life.

4 It lowers cholesterol
Regular exercise brings not only a drop in total cholesterol, but also an improved ratio of "good" HDL cholesterol to "bad" LDL cholesterol.

5 It boosts confidence and body image
People who exercise regularly feel more confident about themselves and have higher self-esteem and a better body image than sedentary people. A study undertaken at La Palestra Center for Preventive Medicine in New York found that people who trained successfully for a marathon noted feeling more motivated, confident, and powerful in other areas of their lives, too.

6 It is associated with a lower risk of some cancers
Research indicates a link between regular exercise and a lower risk of cancer of the breast, womb, lung, and bowel.

7 It lowers the risk of adult-onset diabetes
Regular activity, including resistance training, has been found to increase insulin sensitivity and glucose tolerance. This is particularly welcome news for anyone who may be susceptible to adult-onset diabetes or who is very overweight, since these conditions make the body insensitive to insulin, causing fat to be stored instead of burned.

8 It improves mental function
A Japanese study found that mental faculties such as memory, reaction time, and decision-making abilities were improved after strenuous exercise, probably owing to an increased blood flow to the brain.

9 It enables you to control your weight
Regular exercisers are less likely to be overweight, less likely to gain weight as they get older, and less susceptible to decline in muscle mass and metabolic rate.

10 It makes you happier
Experts are so convinced about the mood-enhancing benefits of exercise that it has been prescribed in cases of mild to moderate depression. Regular exercisers are also more optimistic in nature than couch potatoes.

Stay, or get, active — and you'll be fitter and healthier in mind and body.

THE MUSCULOSKELETAL SYSTEM USE IT OR LOSE IT

When it comes to the musculoskeletal system—bones, muscles, tendons, and ligaments—the old adage "use it or lose it" could not be more appropriate. To remain strong, bones and muscles need to be challenged, or "stressed." Challenge them, and they will adapt; let them do nothing, and they will adapt to that, too. Studies in which volunteers took to their beds for up to two months have shown that bone density and muscle strength deteriorate rapidly when the body has no need to move, and the level of deterioration is directly related to the length of inactivity. On the other hand, strength gains of up to 74 percent have been recorded in previously sedentary people who take up regular exercise—with incremental improvements of up to 5 percent per session.

Most forms of exercise have a positive effect on the musculoskeletal system, but to stimulate strength gains (and muscle toning), resistance exercise is most effective. If you balance this with flexibility training, it will help maintain good mobility and prevent muscles from getting short and tight.

THE CARDIOVASCULAR SYSTEM KEEP IT HEALTHY

The cardiovascular system consists of the heart and the blood vessels that transport blood to and from the heart. There is substantial evidence that regular aerobic exercise improves cardiovascular health and lowers the risk of cardiovascular disease. It achieves these benefits by reducing blood pressure, improving blood vessel elasticity, increasing cardiac output (the amount of blood pumped out by the heart each minute), reducing total cholesterol, and—even better—by increasing the ratio of "good" HDL cholesterol and controlling body weight. There is also evidence that physical activity may prevent stroke. While walking or other low-intensity exercise is good, more vigorous activity, such as running, is associated with a greater risk reduction, according to research published in the *Journal of the American Medical Association*.

GET IN BETTER SHAPE THROUGH PHYSICAL ACTIVITY

Every process that takes place in our bodies, from digestion to muscular movement, requires energy, which is measured in calories (or, strictly, kilocalories/kcal). We obtain the energy from our food, in the form of carbohydrates, fats, or proteins. Foods are broken down, usually in the presence of oxygen, and the constituent parts are used to release stored energy from the body's "energy molecule," known as "ATP." The amount of energy we need each day simply to keep ticking over—even if we don't get out of bed—is referred to as the basal metabolic rate.

We use up additional energy, over and above the basal metabolic rate, through digestion and daily activity. The more active individuals are, the more calories they will burn on a daily basis, which makes it far easier to control their weight. Regular aerobic exercise, such as swimming or cycling, burns plenty of calories.

That information may not come as a particular surprise—but what is not so widely acknowledged is that strength training is another essential constituent of the weight-control jigsaw. While you may not burn a large number of calories from doing push-ups or lifting weights, you are increasing your muscle mass while engaged in this kind of exercise—and since muscle is a very energy-hungry tissue, the more you have, the more energy you will burn, even at rest.

What's more, over time, aerobic exercise enhances your ability to mobilize and use fat as a fuel, so your body becomes a more efficient fat-burning machine.

That is why a combination of aerobic exercise and strength training, coupled with regular flexibility work, is your best bet for all-round fitness.

Sounds like a lot? Think of it in this way. There are 168 hours in a week. Surely it should not be difficult to set aside 3 to 4 hours out of 168. But even if it is, don't be put off. If you only have 10 minutes to spare, then 10 minutes is fine. Every little bit helps—so do what you can, when you can.

TRACK YOUR PROGRESS TO GREATER FITNESS

If you want to get somewhere, you have to know where you are to start with. A few simple tests will put you in picture regarding your current fitness level. When you have completed the first six-week segment of your fitness program (see "My Journal," page 57), reassess yourself on any or all of the tests described below—including the Rockport Walking Test overleaf—to see how you have improved. At the end of each six-week segment, you can fill in the results of any tests you repeat on the pull-out chart.

BMI (body mass index) is a simple way of assessing your body-weight status. It is not perfect, since it does not distinguish between fat and muscle, but it does allow you to get an idea of whether you are a healthy weight. (BMI is assessed according to height in meters and weight in kilograms; to convert inches to meters, multiply by 0.025; to convert pounds to kilograms, multipy by 0.45.)

Body fat can be assessed in a number of ways. It can be measured using skinfold callipers, bioelectrical impedance, or hydrostatic weighing. Most health clubs or gyms are able to offer one of the first two methods, but make sure you get measured by the same person each time for skinfold assessment, as technique variations will affect the reading.

Resting heart rate represents the number of times your heart beats each minute to pump blood around the body when you are at rest. It is measured as beats per minute (bpm). Since a strong cardiovascular system allows you to pump more blood with every beat, your resting heart rate will drop as you get fitter. Measure your heart rate before you even get out of bed or eat or drink anything. Breathe evenly and normally and place two fingers (not your thumb) on the thumb-side of your inner wrist. Count the number of beats you feel in 60 seconds, counting the first beat as zero. Repeat the test, add the results of both tests together, and divide by two for a more representative reading.

MEASURING UP

HEIGHT IN METERS

WEIGHT IN KILOGRAMS

BMI (BODY MASS INDEX)

write down your height in meters and your weight in kilograms; then divide your weight by your height squared: $W/H^2 = BMI$

UNDERWEIGHT =	UNDER 20
NORMAL WEIGHT =	20–24.9
OVERWEIGHT =	25–29.9
VERY OVERWEIGHT =	30+

BODY FAT PERCENTAGE

RESTING HEART RATE (BPM)

MEASUREMENTS (INCHES OR CENTIMETERS)

CHEST

measure with the tape flat across the nipple line

WAIST

measure around the narrowest part of your midriff

NAVEL

measure around the midriff directly over the bellybutton

HIPS

measure across the top of the buttock cheeks

THIGHS

standing with feet together, measure 8in (20cm) up from the top of your kneecap and take a circumference measurement of your thighs

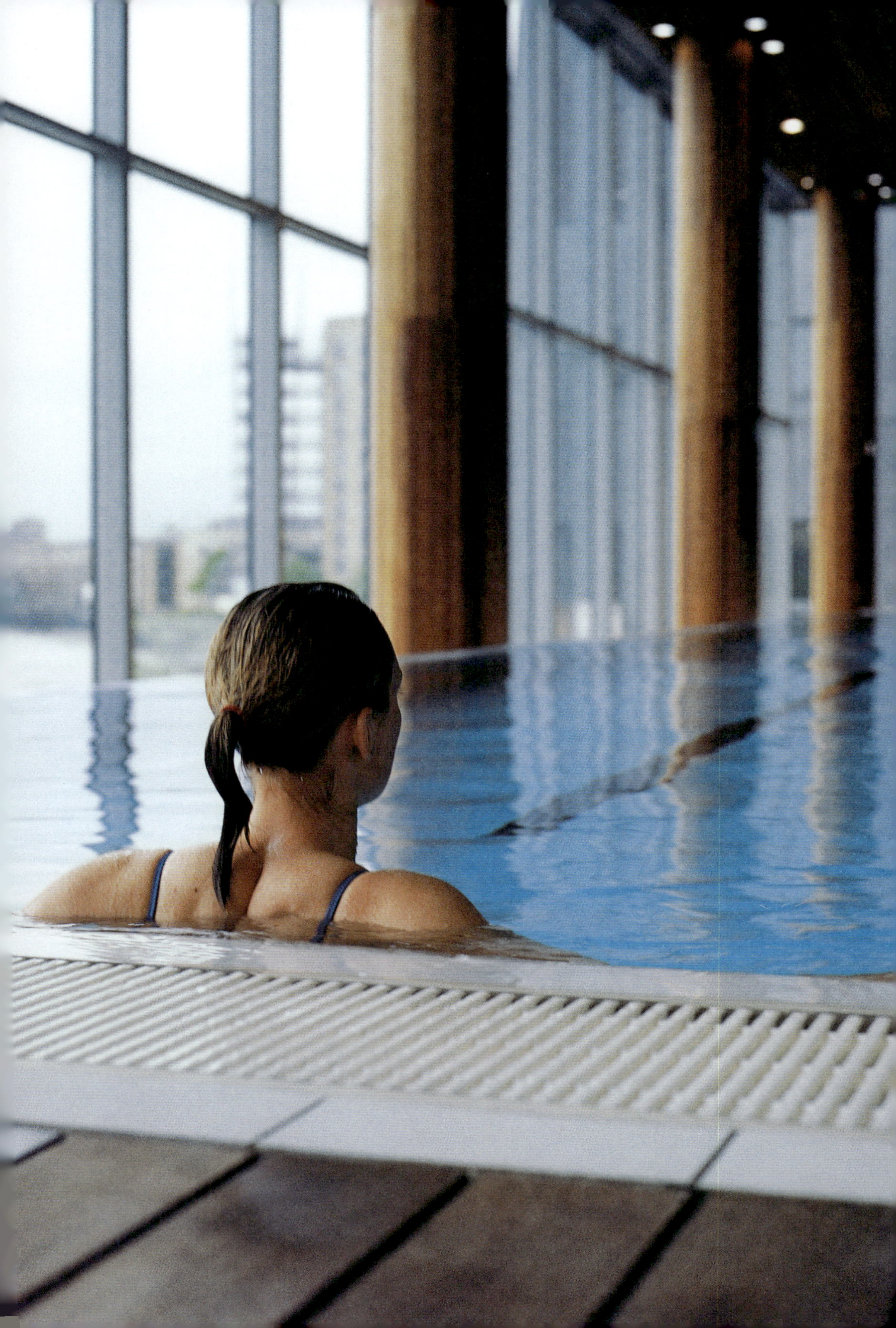

THE ROCKPORT 1-MILE WALKING TEST

The Rockport Walking Test is a way of testing your aerobic fitness. The result is an estimate of your maximal oxygen uptake: the amount of oxygen your body can consume and utilize in the working muscles per minute.

Mark out a flat, obstacle-free course of 1 mile (1,609 meters, or 4 laps of a standard athletics track). Walk the course as fast as you can, recording your time with a stopwatch, and immediately on finishing, record your heart rate for 1 minute, as described on page 14.

Now get a calculator and feed your results into the following equation (to convert kilograms to pounds, multiply by 2.2):
133 − (0.17 x your weight in pounds) − (0.38 x your age in years) + 6.3 for males or 0 for females − (3.26 x time walk took in minutes) − (0.1565 x heart rate/bpm)

Example: You are a 30-year-old female who weighs 130 pounds. You took 14 minutes to walk the course and your heart rate at the end was 137 beats per minute (bpm).
133 − (0.17 x 130) − (0.38 x 30) + 0 − (3.26 x 14) − (0.1565 x 137) =
133 − 22.1 − 11.4 + 0 − 45.64 − 21.44 = 39.26

Results _____
_____
_____
_____

COMPARE YOUR RESULTS WITH THE VALUES SHOWN BELOW

FEMALE

AGE	VERY POOR	POOR	FAIR	GOOD	EXCELLENT	SUPERIOR
20-29	23.6	23.6–28.9	29–32.9	33–36.9	37–41	41
30-39	22.8	22.8–26.9	27–31.4	31.5–35.6	35.7–40	40
40-49	21	21–24.4	24.5–28.9	29–32.8	32.9–36.9	36.9
50-59	20.2	20.2–22.7	22.8–26.9	27–31.4	31.5–35.7	35.7
60+	17.5	17.5–20.1	20.2–24.4	24.5–30.2	30.3–31.4	31.4

MALE

AGE	VERY POOR	POOR	FAIR	GOOD	EXCELLENT	SUPERIOR
20-29	33	33–36.4	36.5–42.4	42.5–46.4	46.5–52.4	52.4
30-39	31.5	31.5–35.4	35.5–40.9	41–44.9	45–49.4	49.4
40-49	30.2	30.2–33.5	33.6–38.9	39–43.7	43.8–48	48
50-59	26.1	26.1–30.9	31–35.7	35.8–40.9	41–45.3	45.3
60+	20.5	20.5–26	26.1–32.2	32.3–36.4	36.5–44.2	44.2

MY EXERCISE PROGRAM

MY EXERCISE PROGRAM

THE BUILDING BLOCKS OF FITNESS

There is no single definition of fitness. For some people, it simply means being fit enough to enjoy daily living, with energy to spare and ease of movement; for others, it may mean running a marathon, being a great tennis player, or sculpting muscles to perfection. No doubt you have very specific goals and aspirations relating to your own fitness, but it is important to address all the major components of fitness rather than just one (such as aerobic fitness) in order to gain a range of health and body benefits, reduce the risk of injury, and achieve a balanced program.

So what are the major building blocks to a fit and healthy body? They are often described as the "three Ss": stamina, strength, and suppleness (or flexibility, to use the more formal term). Different sports—and exercise activities—address different aspects of fitness.

Picture a professional ballet dancer and a soccer player. The ballet dancer is slight of build, yet lean and strong, with astounding flexibility and balance. The footballer has to balance speed and explosive power with endurance and agility. Put one in the other's shoes, and—in spite of their apparent "fitness"—each would no doubt struggle to excel in the other's activity.

But don't worry; getting fit doesn't entail taking up half a dozen sports at a time! What it does mean is that, whatever your preferred form of activity, you should include a little variety to make sure your program is balanced. Other aspects of fitness—such as speed, power, agility, and core stability—are examined later in the chapter.

Finally, a word on technique. Whether you are taking up yoga, weight training, running, or step aerobics, the importance of good technique cannot be stressed enough. Focus on maintaining good posture throughout your workout, and never strain so much that your technique is compromised. Common examples of poor technique include using momentum to lift a heavier weight, "bouncing" to get farther in a stretch, and propping yourself up against machinery to make the workload easier. Don't be tempted!

> "Fitness can be neither bought nor bestowed. Like honor, it must be earned."
> ANON

STAMINA FOR A BETTER QUALITY OF LIFE

In terms of health, stamina—built up through aerobic exercise—is perhaps the most valuable fitness asset to strive for. Aerobic fitness—or, more correctly, cardiorespiratory fitness—relates to the efficiency of the heart and lungs.

People who are aerobically fit are not only more competent at getting through an aerobics class without giving up; they are also able to deal with ordinary tasks, stresses, and strains without feeling burned out by the end of the day. But despite the name, you don't need to "do aerobics" to get aerobically fit. Star jumps and grapevines are fine if they are your thing, but if they are not, you can gain and maintain stamina through any number of activities, especially ones that use the large muscles of the legs and body, require substantial amounts of oxygen, and are prolonged and repetitive—for example, walking briskly, running, dancing, swimming, cycling, or using machines such as the stepper or cross-trainer in a gym.

The harder you work during aerobic exercise, the more calories you will burn, but there is a balance to be achieved between intensity and duration. If you can work hard for only 10 minutes, but you could work slightly less hard for 20 minutes, then go for the more moderate pace to start with. Not only will you be able to clock up more exercise minutes that way, it will also make exercising feel more comfortable (and therefore more pleasurable)—and just as importantly, it will allow your body to adapt more gradually, minimizing the risk of injury or overdoing it.

WORKING OUT FOR MORE STAMINA

Since cardiorespiratory fitness is so important to health, experts recommend that we aim to get 30 minutes a day of aerobic activity on most days of the week. It does not need to be all in one burst—some studies have shown that breaking exercise down into mini sessions of approximately 10 minutes will burn more calories (kilocalories/kcal) than doing one prolonged session.

If you want to go beyond merely safeguarding your health, aim to work a little harder in some of your aerobic activities. The American College of Sports Medicine recommends 2 to 5 sessions of more vigorous exercise, lasting 20 to 50 minutes. But don't get started until you have read about the principles of training, and learned how to warm up, cool down, and stretch (see pages 26–27 and 34–40).

The energy expenditure of some common aerobic activities is shown below. The figures are based on a 137lb (62kg) woman performing one hour of the activity. If you weigh less, the value will be lower; if you weigh more, it will be higher.

Activity	kcal	Activity	kcal
CIRCUIT TRAINING	385 KCAL	CROSS-COUNTRY SKIING	530 KCAL
CYCLING (MODERATE TO BRISK PACE)	375 KCAL	ROWING (MODERATE PACE)	440 KCAL
HIGH IMPACT AEROBICS	385 KCAL	SWIMMING (MODERATE FRONT CRAWL)	500 KCAL
SKIPPING	610 KCAL	SWIMMING (FAST BREAST STROKE)	600 KCAL
ROLLERBLADING	400 KCAL	TENNIS (RECREATIONAL)	410 KCAL
JOGGING (9-MINUTE-MILE PACE)	675 KCAL	BRISK WALKING (15-MINUTE-MILE PACE)	360 KCAL
RUNNING (7-MINUTE-MILE PACE)	900 KCAL		

"Everyone is an athlete. The only difference is that some of us are training, and some are not."

Dr George Sheehan, cardiologist and runner

STRENGTH FOR THE BODY BEAUTIFUL

The importance of strength training reaches far beyond such obvious goals as gaining bulky muscles or being able to move heavy objects.

Performed regularly, strength training will reward you with a faster metabolism, less body fat, a sleeker, firmer physique, and stronger connective tissues and bones. There is also an increasing amount of evidence to suggest that weight training can favorably modify several risk factors for heart disease and diabetes, including lipid and cholesterol levels, blood pressure, body composition—that is, the ration of body fat to muscle—and glucose metabolism.

One thing strength training does not do is burn many calories. But while it will not elevate your heart rate enough to stoke the calorie furnace while you are actually doing it, the increased muscle mass that you will reap from regular strength training means that your resting metabolic rate will increase—so you will be burning more calories all the time.

Here's how it works. One pound of fat uses just a handful of calories to maintain itself each day. A pound of muscle, however, is far more "energy-hungry," requiring approximately 45 calories a day. So, if you replace 2lb (910g) of fat with 2lb of muscle, you will actually be burning 90 more calories every day, even when you are not exercising.

Strong muscles have more tone and are denser than untrained ones, too, so—even though you may not weigh less according to the scales—you will look and feel firmer and trimmer. Another important benefit of strength training is that it can help to stave off osteoporosis, or loss of bone mass, in later life, because the action of muscle pulling on bone stimulates bone to get stronger.

One study, whose results were published in the *American Journal of Clinical Nutrition*, found that 12 weeks of strength training resulted in 4lb (1.81kg) of fat loss and 3lb (1.36kg) of muscle gain.

WORKING OUT FOR MORE STRENGTH

Strength training is not restricted to lifting weights in a gym. You can perform resistance work with just your own body weight as resistance, or use tubing and elasticated "resistance" bands, hand weights, water bottles, medicine balls, even full tincans!

To make significant strength gains (as well as sculpting and toning your muscles), you will need to work with weights 2 or 3 times a week, but it should not be a long time before you can see satisfying results.

The American Heart Association has published a Scientific Advisory which recommends doing 8 to 15 repetitions of each exercise, and including a variety of 8 to 10 different exercises. That will occupy maybe 20 to 30 minutes. Alternatively, you could try one of the group strength-training classes, such as BodyPump.

SUPPLENESS FOR GRACE AND FLUIDITY

Suppleness, or flexibility, is not about wrapping your legs behind your neck or even touching your toes; it is about having a good range of motion in all your joints, allowing for easy, fluid movement, correct posture, and muscle balance.

Regular stretching increases blood supply and nutrients to joint structures, keeping tissues pliable and elastic, and possibly slowing down the degeneration of the joints. There is also evidence to show that increasing flexibility and range of motion can cut the incidence of lower back pain by reducing stress to the lumbar spine.

Flexibility differs from joint to joint. You may have fantastic hip mobility, for example, while you find it hard to reach your hand around your back to do up a zipper because your shoulders are tight and immobile. That is why it is important to devise and follow a total stretching program (see pages 37–40), rather than simply focusing on one or two muscle groups.

Flexibility naturally declines with age because as we grow older there is more fibrous collagen in the muscles, making them less pliable. Regular flexibility work can help offset the effects of aging and slow down the decline in suppleness. It can also help realign soft tissue structures that have adapted to bad postural habits.

WORKING OUT FOR MORE SUPPLENESS

Activities such as yoga, Pilates, swimming, tai chi, and other martial arts will all help you maintain suppleness by means of the variety of positions and ranges of movement involved. But if your exercise program does not incorporate one of these activities, make time for stretching after your activity, or on alternate days of the week. Stretching is a wonderful way to "switch off" after your workout, and you will find that the deep breathing and slow, gentle movements involved enhance relaxation and bestow a sense of well-being.

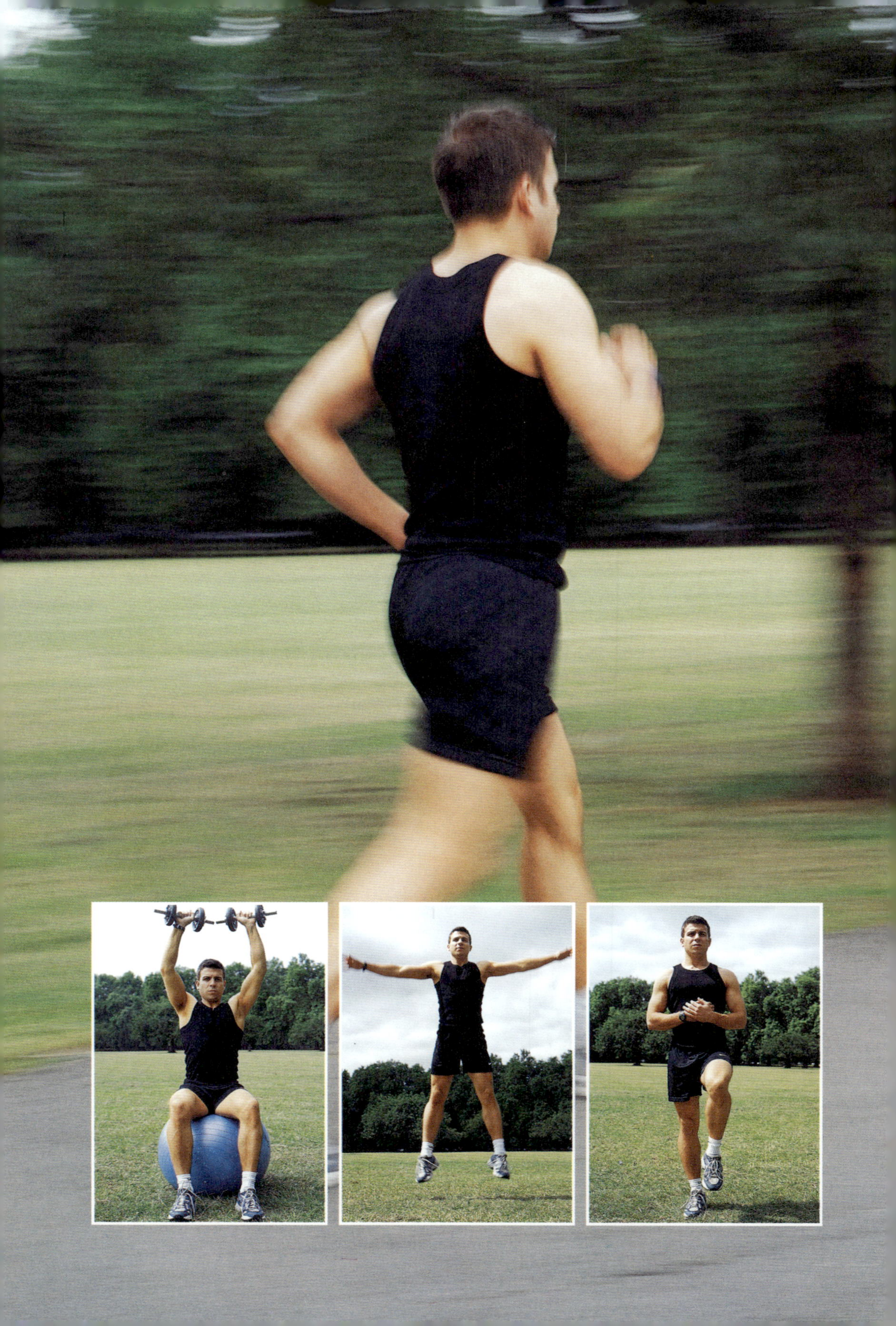

OTHER FITNESS ATTRIBUTES FOR SAFETY AND SUCCESS

Research has shown that many avid gym users have poor core stability, which puts them at risk of injury, back pain, and muscular imbalances. Core stability relates to the strength and responsiveness of the muscles around the back and pelvis (the core), from which all other movement emanates. Other fitness attributes include balance, speed, power, and agility.

Exercises to improve **core stability** are often very subtle, can be repeated several times each day, and usually don't require any external resistance. Improvement is also subtle. It shows itself in greater efficiency of movement, better posture, and an absence of discomfort. Classes that hone core stability include Reebok Core, which uses a special "core board," Pilates, and sessions that involve fit balls (large inflatable balls).

Closely related to core stability is **balance**. This is all about your sense of body awareness and where you are in space. If you stand with your eyes closed and lift one leg off the floor, you will soon start to wobble. The reason is that you rely much more heavily on your visual sense than on your kinesthetic awareness (how a movement feels). Exercise improves body awareness and balance, which helps you move more efficiently, reduces the risk of falls in later life, and enables you to perform better in complex movements and sports. Activities that challenge balance include yoga, ballet, and martial arts. You can also hone your balance at home with a wobble board, fit ball, or stability disc.

Speed is an essential attribute in some sport and fitness activities. You can experiment with speed in your aerobic exercise sessions by adding faster bursts, or breaking up sessions into speed efforts with periods of recovery in between. This will enhance your aerobic fitness as well as give you an edge in competition.

Power reflects the ability to apply a force quickly. Imagine doing a simple squat exercise, and then picture leaping from the squat position up into the air, landing back into a squat. That's power! It is essential to sports such as basketball and athletic events such as long jump or javelin throw. It is also important in activities such as gymnastics and ballet.

Agility is the ability to move fast in all directions. It is a great attribute for most active people since it challenges the nerves and muscles that enable you to move not just in a forward motion (as in running, walking, or cycling) but sideways, backward, up, and down. This gives you a more "rounded" fitness and reduces the risk of injury if you have to move suddenly in a direction you are not accustomed to. Team-sport players know the importance of this skill, but if you do circuits or aerobics, you will also benefit from enhanced agility.

SO WHAT'S THE BEST EXERCISE?

The best exercise is the one you enjoy most and will therefore continue to do, but you should view it in the context of your lifestyle as a whole. For example, if you love yoga, make it your main activity—but make sure you get sufficient aerobic exercise, perhaps by walking to and from the class at a brisk pace. Mountain biking is your thing? Great— you'll be improving your aerobic fitness and leg strength, but include some upper-body and trunk-strength exercises and a full-body stretch for a more balanced program.

THE PRINCIPLES OF TRAINING TAKING IT STEP BY STEP

Once you have decided what type of exercise would be most appropriate for you, the next stage is to think about the details. How much exercise should you do? How quickly should you expect to progress? And how should you plan your exercise week?

1 Make haste slowly

Progressing at the right pace is crucial to the success of any training regime. Say, for example, you started walking regularly four weeks ago. Initially, walking a mile in 15 minutes was a real challenge, but now it feels pretty easy. If you don't walk either faster or farther, the fitness benefits you have gained from walking will tail off. Why? Because your body is no longer being challenged by the activity.

For health and fitness improvements to occur, you must continue to challenge your body with a greater workload. It will only adapt when the challenge placed upon it is greater than that which it can already do. This is known as "progressive overload"—progressive because the overload applied must be increased very gradually. Next time, don't try to walk a mile in 10 minutes, but perhaps you could aim to do it in 14 minutes. Get the overload right and your body will adapt successfully.

The "My Journal" section of this book (see pages 55–140) includes a Taking Stock page to fill in every six weeks. This gives you an opportunity to assess what you have achieved so far. Have you got where you wanted to be? If not, what did you do wrong? Did you manage to fit in as much as you wanted? What kind of changes do you want to make over the next six weeks?

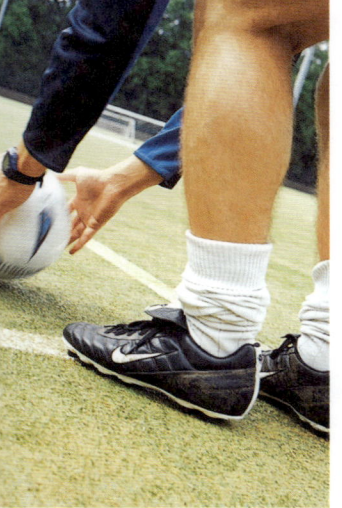

2 Be specific, but not exclusive

If you want to be a marathon runner, you need to work on your endurance. If you want to be a sprinter, you need to hone your speed. Put simply, the principle of "specificity" means do the thing you want to be better at; whatever it is you want to achieve from your fitness program should be its main component. But it is also important to maintain your strength, stamina, and suppleness—so don't neglect the rest in favor of just one.

All work and no play makes Jack a dull boy, and no doubt you would soon find yourself bored if all you ever did was to swim laps or run on the treadmill. Adding variety to your exercise program not only gives your body a wider range of challenges, but also keeps your mind fresh and makes exercise more interesting and fun. And—perhaps most importantly—it reduces the chance of overuse injuries from doing too much of one activity.

3 Take a rest
Here is some good news. A very important part of your fitness program is rest. It is during rest that the body undergoes adaptation (see point 1, opposite), rather than when it is actually exercising, so failing to schedule in "down-time" means that you won't see the results you might expect. Always take one day's break from exercise each week, and after very challenging workouts, schedule in easy days, when you exercise at a lower intensity.

4 Be consistent
The sad fact is, you can't store fitness. It is really important to persevere with regular exercise to maintain the results you have achieved. If you don't progress your routine, or exercise only erratically, the principle of "reversibility" comes into play, and you'll be taking one step forward, two steps back. However, once you have achieved a certain level of fitness, you can maintain it on rather less exercise than it took to get there in the first place. For example, you can maintain strength gains on two days a week, even though it may have taken thrice-weekly sessions to reach that level of strength.

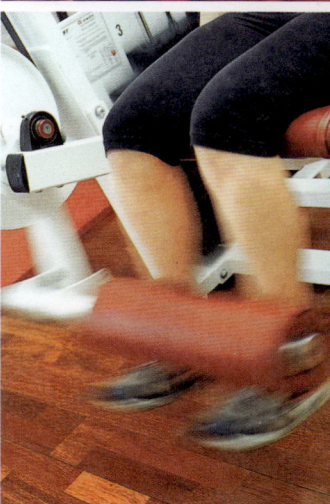

5 Follow the FIT principle
The final thing you need to consider before you are ready to build your workout program is the FIT principle. FIT is all about the how, what, and when of exercise. The golden rule with the FIT principle is: if you increase one, the others should stay the same. For example, if you work harder, don't try to work longer, too. If you add another weekly workout, don't try to increase the length of time of your existing workouts. In general, you should aim to exercise three to six days a week, depending on your goals, current fitness level, and time availability.

THE FIT PRINCIPLE

F — STANDS FOR FREQUENCY
How often are you going to exercise?
I — STANDS FOR INTENSITY
How hard are you going to exercise?
T — STANDS FOR TIME
How long are you going to exercise for?
Or how far are you going to go?

(It makes no difference whether you measure your activity in terms of distance or time, but it is worth keeping track of one or the other so that you have the means to monitor your progress.)

SETTING FITNESS GOALS

Write down your goals, then review them against the checklist below and adapt as necessary.

_____
_____
_____
_____
_____
_____
_____
_____
_____
_____
_____
_____
_____
_____
_____
_____
_____

SMART GOALS CHECKLIST

ARE MY GOALS SPECIFIC? Clue: Instead of "I want to lose weight," try "I want to lose 7lbs (3kg) in the next eight weeks."
ARE MY GOALS MEASURABLE? Clue: Instead of "I want to improve my aerobic fitness," try "I want to be able walk a mile in 14 minutes."
ARE MY GOALS ACHIEVABLE? Clue: Instead of "I want to take up running so I can do the marathon in three months," try "I want to begin a sensible running program so I can build up to running a marathon next year."
ARE MY GOALS RELEVANT? Do they mean something to you? Clue: Instead of "I want to take up yoga because everyone else seems to be trying it," try "I want to learn bellydancing because I've always fancied doing something exotic."
ARE MY GOALS TIME-RELATED? Clue: Instead of "I want to get a flatter stomach," try "I want to get a flatter stomach by the time I go to the beach in six weeks' time."

Once you have written down your SMART goals, consider these points:

Are my goals positively stated?
Never use negative wording when describing your goals—otherwise you will be setting yourself up for failure. Phrases such as "I should," "I must," and "I ought to," are all outlawed, as are "Giving up" and "Stop." Instead of "I want to stop eating so much junk," try "I will make healthier eating choices."

Can I achieve all my goals at once?
Have you taken on too much and put too much pressure on yourself? If so, the solution is to prioritize your goals and focus on one for each six-week segment of the journal (see pages 55–140). Beware of goals that conflict with each other. You will have a much better chance of success if you work on one aspect of your health and fitness at a time rather than trying to change your life all at once.

MY FITNESS PROGRAM

Write down the details of your program, being as specific as you can.

PUT YOUR PROGRAM THROUGH THE REALITY CHECK

Consider the answers to the following questions to make sure you are setting off on the right road with every chance of success.
Does my program have a balance of aerobic activity, strength, and flexibility work? ___
Does my program fit into my existing lifestyle without taking it over? ___
Am I looking forward to starting my program? ___
Do I feel confident that I can stick to my program? ___

If the answer to any of these questions is "No," go back through this section to find out what changes you need to make. You'll find some motivational tips on page 52.

THE BASICS

GETTING OFF ON THE RIGHT FOOT

A workout should start with a warm-up, end with a cool-down, and be followed by a stretch. This chapter explains how to get this routine right, but it starts by looking at good posture—the basis from which all exercise should begin. Good posture can feel strange because most of us fail to achieve it most of the time.

Try this posture-perfecting exercise. Stand with feet slightly apart. Make sure the weight is evenly spaced between the front and back of the feet, and between the left and right feet. Soften your knees and pull up through the legs. Keep the hips square and level. Imagine your pelvic girdle is a bucketful of water, and don't let it tip either forward or back. Lengthen through the spine and contract the abdominal muscles, gently pulling the belly button toward the spine as you extend tall. Drop the rib cage, pulling the lower ribs toward the pubic bone. Relax the shoulders and gently open the chest and front of the shoulders by turning your hands to face your thighs. Keep the neck long, and let the shoulders "float" back and the head sit on top of the spine. Make sure the buttocks are unclenched and the backs of the knees are relaxed. Breathe freely.

If you want to assess your current posture, stand side on to a mirror and march on the spot for a few seconds, with eyes closed. Let your body come to a natural standstill. Now open your eyes and take a look—or, better still, get a friend or partner to assess you in profile and from the front. Watch out for the following faults:

head Is the head jutting forward or tilting to the left or right? Is the chin slightly lifted?
shoulders Are the shoulders rounded or hunched? Check each shoulder separately.
hands Are the palms facing back?
upper back Is the upper back excessively rounded?
lower back Is the lower back excessively concave or flat? Does the bottom jut out?
stomach Does the stomach protrude and the pelvis tip back?
hipbones Are the hipbones level—or is there more weight on one side than the other?
knees Do the knees point either out to the sides or toward each other?
feet Is the weight mainly in the heels or balls, or more on one foot than the other?

> "Intelligent training is knowing the why of an exercise, as well as the what and how."
>
> ARTHUR LYDIARD,
> FORMER TOP MARATHON RUNNER AND COACH

WARMING UP WHY AND HOW

There are some activities that you wouldn't dream of starting without a warm-up—basketball, ballet, or running, for example. But, if you are going for a swim, the chances are you spend no time at all limbering up or loosening the joints before you hit the pool; if you are taking a hike, you simply set off. The fact is, whatever your sport or activity, there are great reasons to warm up. (Hint: How many elite athletes have you seen forgo a warm-up?)

The amount of oxygen your body needs during exercise can be as much as five times the amount it needs at rest. If you were to leap off the sofa and plunge straight into a challenging workout, your body would have a hard time meeting the increased oxygen demand, and you would feel pretty uncomfortable. In contrast, if you start slowly, your body has time to adapt by increasing the heart rate and the amount of blood being directed to the working muscles. In addition, when muscles are cold, they are less pliant and more liable to tear, while joints are not wholly lubricated—it is movement itself that "greases" the joint surfaces.

A warm-up prepares you not only physically but also psychologically for the activity you are about to perform—making it like a mental rehearsal for the workout. Preparing your mind increases mind–body synergy, and enhances nerve–muscle coordination (particularly important in technical sports and complex movements).

WHAT DO I DO?

Start with some gentle rhythmic, circling mobilizations of the major joints of the body, including the neck, shoulders, waist, hips, knees, and ankles. Follow this with some light aerobic work to increase body temperature, heart rate, and blood flow. Marching on the spot, walking, and gentle cycling are all good options.

COOLING DOWN WHY AND HOW

When your workout is complete, don't stop suddenly. In the same way that warming up prepares your body for exercise, cooling down prepares it to return to a resting state. Your workout will have raised your heart rate and body temperature considerably, and it is important to allow these to begin to return to normal before you stop. This will prevent you from feeling dizzy or lightheaded, and will encourage your body to remove waste products from the muscles and aid your recovery from the workout. It will also help you relax after your exertions.

WHAT DO I DO?

The best form of cool-down is a slower version of the activity you have been performing. So, if you have been cycling, swimming, or running, for example, spend a few minutes doing the activity really slowly and with very little effort. Alternatively, simply walk or march on the spot, and then repeat some of the mobilizations you did in the warm-up. Your body temperature will drop quite quickly, so make sure you put on an extra layer of clothing, or have a warm bath or shower, before you progress to the next essential: stretching.

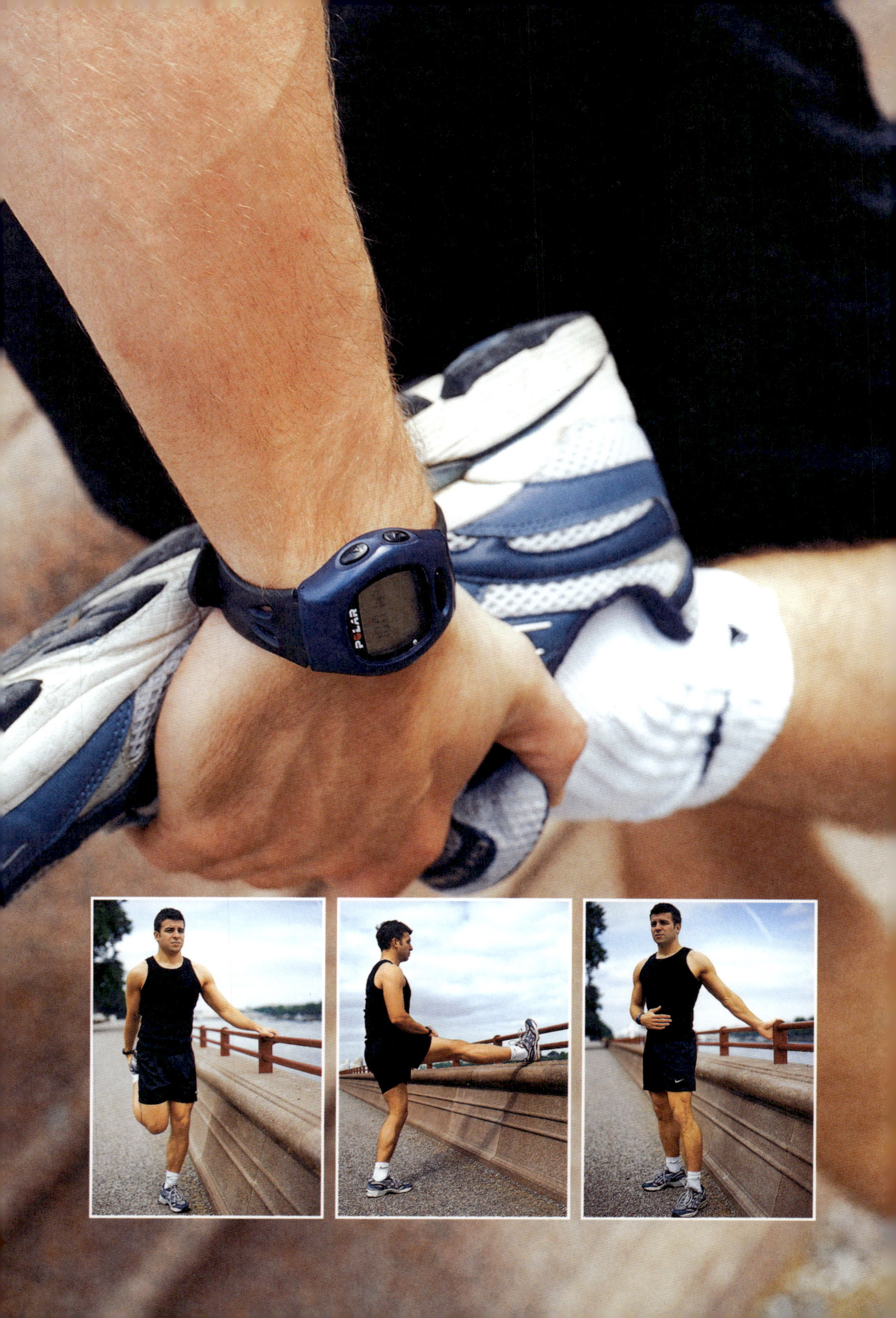
POLAR

STRETCHING WHY AND HOW

There has been some recent controversy about the purpose and value of stretching—with some experts saying that it is a waste of time because it doesn't, as was once claimed, reduce the risk of injury or improve performance in a sport.

This new way of thinking may have some validity. But consider the effects of daily life—and regular workouts—on your physical condition. For example, if you have a sedentary job, or one in which you repeat similar movement patterns all day long, it is likely that your body has adapted to this demand by making some muscles stronger and allowing others to get weaker. Your range of movement in some joints, the ones you use frequently, is probably fine, while other joints, those that are put through their paces less often, have become less mobile.

Add to this general wear and tear the natural decline in flexibility that comes with aging—a decline that in some people starts from as young as the age of 20!—as well as the extra imbalances and demands placed on muscles and joints by exercise, and you can see why stretching may be worthwhile after all.

Muscles contract and shorten during exercise. One purpose of stretching is to restore them to their optimal length. In addition, if a joint has been put through only a limited range of movement during an activity—for example, the low leg lift involved in jogging does not put the knee through its full range—it is important after the activity to put the joint through its full range. If you fail to do so, your mobility will gradually deteriorate.

To establish which stretching exercises are most appropriate for your sport, select one or more types of sport from the table below and match the colors beside them with the color codes assigned to each of the stretches described in this section.

MATCH YOUR SPORT WITH THE COLOR-CODED STRETCHES

Colors	Sport	Colors	Sport
■ ■ □	weight training	■ ■	jogging or running
■ ■ □	circuit training	■	rollerblading
■ ■ □	rowing	■	aerobics/step aerobics
■ ■ □	swimming	■	step machine/cross trainer
■ ■ □	skipping	■	skiing/cross-country skiing
■ ■ □	tennis	■	walking
■ ■ □	martial arts	■ □	surfing
■ ■ □	kickboxing	■ □	rock climbing
■ ■ □	water aerobics	■ □	golf
■ ■ □	yoga	■ □	throwing sports, such as javelin and discus
■ ■ □	tai chi		
■ ■ □	basketball, netball, volleyball, and other court sports	■ ■	road cycling
		■ ■	mountain biking
■ ■ □	dance workouts	■ ■	soccer and other field sports

■ lower-body stretch　　■ back and torso stretch　　□ upper-body stretch

Hamstrings

Stand in front of a support that is between knee and hip height. Extend your right leg and place it on the support, with the foot relaxed. You should be at a distance from the support that allows the left leg to be perpendicular to the floor. Resting your hands on your hips, hinge forward from the hips, keeping the pelvis level and the right knee straight. Feel the stretch along the back of the thigh. Repeat with left leg.

Quadriceps

Stand tall with feet parallel and lift the right heel, taking your right hand behind you to grab the foot and bring it toward your bottom. Keeping the pelvis in a neutral position and knees close together, gently press the foot into your hand. As long as you feel a stretch, it doesn't matter if your stretching thigh is in front of the supporting one (this indicates tightness). Repeat with left side.

Hip flexors

Adopt a lunge position on the floor: with the right foot forward, take your left knee to the floor with the lower leg extended behind it, and adjust your position so that your pelvis is in neutral and your right leg bent at a right angle. You can support yourself with your hands on the floor or on the front thigh (not on the knee). Feel a stretch along the front of the left thigh and hip. Repeat with left foot forward and right knee to the floor.

Calves (two stretches)

Standing in front of a wall or bar, take a lunge forward with the left leg, keeping the right leg straight out behind you, heel on the floor. Both feet should both be pointing directly forward. Use the wall for support and keep your pelvis in line with your back (the buttocks should not stick out). Repeat with the other leg. Next, stand on a step with your right heel overlapping the back edge of it. Bend at the knees and hips and, keeping most of your weight on the left leg, gently press the right heel down, simultaneously pulling the toes up. Repeat with left heel.

Outer thighs

Sit on the floor with legs outstretched. Bend your right knee, cross the right leg over the left leg, and place the right foot on the floor close to the back of the left thigh. Wrap your left arm around the bent leg and gently turn the torso until you feel a stretch along the outer right thigh. Repeat with left leg.

Inner thighs

Sit up tall, with the soles of your feet together and your hands wrapped loosely around your feet. Gently press down on the inside of the knee or thighs with your elbows to open the legs, creating a stretch along the inner thighs.

Gluteals

Lie on your back and bring your right knee close into your chest, hands wrapped around the shin, the knee fully bent. Hold the position, release, then bring the knee across the body toward the left shoulder, and hold again. Repeat with left leg.

Lower back (two stretches)

Begin on all fours, hands under shoulders, knees under hips, and head in line with spine. Extend the spine by hollowing the back gently, opening the chest, lifting the head, and tilting back the hip bones.
Pause, then go back through the starting position to form a rounded shape, dropping the head, opening the back of the shoulders and tucking the hips under. Gently pull in the abdomen.

☐ Side stretch

Stand with your feet hip-distance apart and arms by your sides. Let your right hand travel down your right leg as you allow the entire torso to drop to the right, feeling a stretch along the left side. Pause, then return to the start position and repeat on the left side. To increase the stretch, perform the exercise with your hands linked above your head.

☐ Upper back

Clasp your hands together with the palms facing your body and push the arms away from you, feeling a stretch along the back of the shoulders and upper back. Try to make your upper back into a 'C' shape.

☐ Triceps

Raise your right arm over your head and let it drop down behind your back. Then take the left hand up and gently push the right elbow back until you feel a stretch along the back of the right arm. Repeat with left arm.

☐ Shoulders

Bring your right arm across your body, just below shoulder height, and—holding the right arm above the elbow—use your left hand to gently press the arm toward the chest. Don't hunch your shoulder. Repeat with left arm.

Chest ☐

Stand in a doorway with your right foot in front of your left and your right arm bent at shoulder level, the forearm resting against the doorframe. Then gently lean through the doorway until you feel a stretch along the front of the chest and right shoulder. Turn around and repeat the stretch on the left.

Neck ☐

Sit or stand tall, and take your head directly to the right side, not allowing it to tilt up or down. To increase the stretch, extend the left arm, pointing fingers toward the floor. Repeat on the other side.

MY NUTRITION

FUEL FOR EXERCISE

The energy that fuels our fitness workouts—not to mention the process of daily living—comes from the food and drink we consume, in the form of carbohydrates, fats, proteins, and, to a lesser extent, alcohol. All of these contain calories, but each contains a different number of calories per gram: carbohydrate 4, fat 9, protein 4, and alcohol 7.

Few of the foods we regularly consume are made up exclusively of one type of fuel; most of them contain a mixture of, say, protein and fat, or carbohydrate and fat. The overall energy content (kcal value) of a food is the sum total of each component it contains. From the comparative figures given above for carbohydrate, fat, protein, and alcohol it is immediately obvious why fatty foods and alcohol should be used sparingly. Not only can they be harmful to health if taken in excess, but they are also provide the quickest way to notch up calorie intake and increase the risk of becoming overweight.

However, any nutrient that is eaten in excess will result in weight gain. This is because both carbohydrate and protein can be converted to body fat if the energy they provide is not required. To find out how much energy you need each day to maintain your present weight, do the calculations on page 44. If you want to lose weight, aim to cut your daily intake of calories by 15 percent; this will ensure you still have all the energy you need for exercise while facilitating weight loss.

Before embarking on any weight-control program, take a minute to read about the role each of the main nutrients performs in the body (see pages 46–48); this information will enable you to maintain a balanced healthy diet, whether you are hoping to lose, gain, or maintain your weight.

Finally, a word about portion sizes. Recent research from the University of North Carolina found that food portion sizes have increased over the last decade both inside and outside the home. Restaurant portions can provide as much as three times the number of calories you would get from a standard portion. Share portions with your friends or partner, ask for a smaller serving, or leave what you don't want.

> "It's good food, and not fine words, that keeps me alive."
> MOLIÈRE (1622–73)

CALCULATING CALORIES

The amount of energy you require each day is determined by your resting metabolic rate (RMR)—the minimum number of calories needed to survive—plus the amount of extra energy you need to perform your daily routine, whether that consists of running around after your children, doing a physical job, or working out to your favorite exercise video. If you want to get a rough idea of how many calories you need to maintain your current weight, do the following calculations.

HOW MANY CALORIES DO I NEED?

1 My weight in kilograms (to convert pounds to kilograms, multiply by 0.45).

2 I am a woman between the ages of 18 and 30:
     weight x 14.7. Answer + 496 =RMR
   I am a woman between the ages of 31 and 60:
     weight x 8.7. Answer + 829 = RMR
   I am a man between the ages of 18 and 30:
     weight x 15.3. Answer + 679 =RMR
   I am a man between the ages of 31 and 60:
     weight x 11.6. Answer + 879 =RMR

3 Take this figure and multiply it by the number below that most closely represents your typical daily activity level.
   I am sedentary (sit or stand most of the day)   1.4
   I am moderately active (some walking each day
   and regular active leisure-time activities)   1.7
   I am very active (physically active each day)   2.0

4 Now add up the number of calories you expend on exercise in a typical week (see the table of activities on page 20 for an estimate), and divide that number by 7 to get a daily figure.

5 Add the results from 3 and 4 together, to give you a rough estimate of how much energy you need per day to maintain your current weight.

RESULTS

_____

_____

_____

_____

STAYING ACTIVE, LOSING WEIGHT

If you want to lose weight, you need to create a calorie deficit by consuming fewer than the number of calories required to maintain your present weight.

Alternatively, you can increase the amount of energy expended on exercise by becoming more active. The ideal solution is to reduce your energy intake a little and increase your energy expenditure. That way, you don't have to make enormous life changes, but you will soon achieve the results you want.

You may have heard that low-intensity exercise burns more fat than high-intensity exercise—and may therefore have decided that, for weight-loss purposes, you would be better off keeping your workouts at a fairly low intensity. As shown by the following example, this is not the case. If you exercise for half an hour at a low intensity—by, say, jogging at a pace of 15 minutes per mile—you may burn roughly 400 calories in an hour, with approximately 60 percent of the total calories coming from body fat. If you exercise for half an hour at a higher intensity—by, say, jogging at a pace of 8 minutes per mile— you would burn closer to 700 calories in an hour, but only 40 percent of the total calories would come from body fat. So, as you can see, a higher intensity workout results in the burning of more calories overall—which is what really counts.

CARBOHYDRATES THE BODY'S PREFERRED FUEL

Carbohydrates are the body's preferred fuel—and the only fuel that can be utilized by the brain—but we need to choose our body's carbohydrate sources carefully.

The majority of the calories we consume—55 to 65 percent of total calories—should come from carbohydrate sources, such as whole grains, starchy vegetables, pulses (also known as legumes) and fruit, pasta, rice, and cereal. Those foods that release their energy slowly, such as brown rice and oatmeal, have what is known as a low "glycemic index" (GI), while refined starches, such as white bread and rice, cause a sharp rise and fall in blood sugar and have a high glycemic index. High glycemic foods can create energy highs and lows, causing us to snack unnecessarily or forgo workouts because we feel tired—so opt for lower GI foods where possible.

While it is not possible to deduce a food's GI simply from its appearance (partly because other nutrients, such as fat or protein, or compounds such as fiber, influence how quickly or slowly a food's energy can be released), learning the GI rating of foods you eat regularly can help you maintain steady energy levels.

GLYCEMIC INDEX TABLE

LOW GI (BELOW 50)	MODERATE GI (50–70)	HIGH GI (70+)
oatmeal	banana	baked potato
yogurt	corn	bread (white or whole-wheat)
lentils	new potatoes (boiled)	honey
orange juice	Special K	sports drinks
spaghetti	brown rice	white rice
apple	Ryvita	carrots
dried apricots	stoneground whole-wheat bread	watermelon
kidney beans	raisins	bagel
chocolate	pineapple	gelatin candy
baked beans	strawberry preserve	french bread

PROTEINS THE "BUILDING BLOCKS" OF LIFE

Protein is not one of the body's major fuel suppliers—consumption of protein should constitute about 15 percent of our overall energy intake.

When your muscles' carbohydrate stores are depleted, or when you are not eating enough carbohydrate, protein can be broken down to produce energy, reflecting its role as a "building block" for muscles and other organs. The average sedentary person is recommended to consume 0.75g of protein per kg (the equivalent of about ¼ oz per 21lb) of body weight each day, while people who regularly strength-train or take part in heavy physical training are advised to consume 1.2–1.4g per kg per day. If you are moderately active, aim for between 0.75 and 1.2g per kg. Good sources include poultry, lean meat, lowfat dairy products, eggs, fish, tofu, pulses (legumes), and nuts.

FATS VITAL NUTRIENTS THAT NEED MONITORING

The average UK diet consists of 40 percent fat—significantly higher than the maximum 30 percent recommended for good health. In the USA, 35 percent of daily calories come from fat, a reduction from 40 percent since the 1960s, but still in excess of health guidelines. In addition, too much of the fat we eat comes from unhealthy saturated and transfat sources (derived from meat and dairy products, pastry, fried food, cakes, and cookies) and not enough comes from healthier, monounsaturated fat (such as olive oil) and sources of the two essential fatty acids, Omega-3 and Omega-6, such as oily fish.

However, just because low fat is good, it doesn't mean no fat is better. Aiming for a daily fat intake between 20–30 percent of total calories—with no more than 10 percent of total calories from saturated fat and a bare minimum of transfats—will help you maintain a healthy body weight and significantly improve the health of your heart.

Fat is an important nutrient for health; it protects our organs, plays a role in enabling and sustaining pregnancy, and helps keep us warm. Some vitamins—A, D, E, and K—depend on the presence of fat to be broken down and used within the body.

FAT FACTS

- Good sources of monounsaturated fats include olive oil, rapeseed oil, and nut oils.
- The two most important polyunsaturated fats are the "essential fatty acids" Omega-3 (found in oily fish, flaxseed, hempseed, walnuts and their oils, canola and soybean oils, and, to a lesser extent, green leafy vegetables) and Omega-6 (derived from seed oils, corn oil, nuts, and wheatgerm). Since we are unable to manufacture these fats in the body, they have to be obtained from food.
- Foods high in transfats include anything in which vegetable oil has been hydrogenated, such as margarine, shortening, fried foods, breads, crackers, snack foods, spreads, and processed/prepared foods.
- Foods high in saturated fat include meat (especially red meat), dairy foods, and palm oil.

DRINK UP

Although it is calorie-free and nutritionally empty, water is a vital part of our diet. It is involved in every bodily process, from energy metabolism to digestion and muscle contraction, and makes up almost two-thirds of our body composition.

We need 2500ml (more than 5 pints) of fluid per day for optimal functioning, and almost a third of that is derived from solid food. The rest comes from the fluids we drink, including juice, soft drinks, coffee, and tea, but it is advisable to drink at least some plain water because—in addition to being free of sugar, caffeine, and calories—it is good for health. (Please note that pint measurements in this section refer to US pints.)

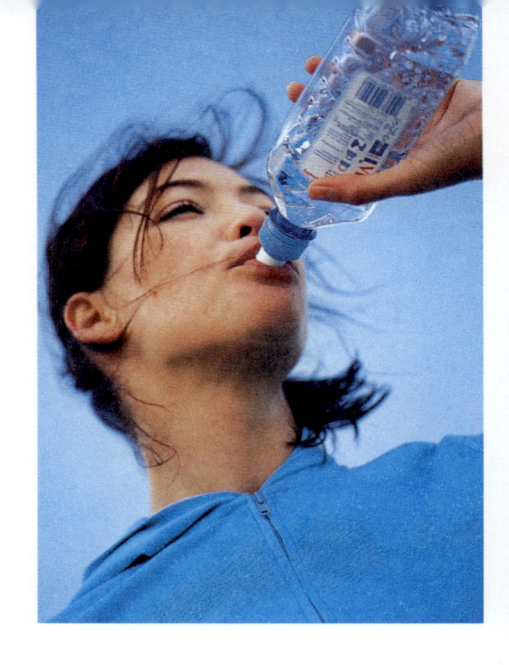

When you are taking regular exercise, you need to replace the fluid you lose through sweating by drinking more than you would at rest. Research carried out by the University Medical School in Aberdeen, Scotland, shows that marathon runners lose up to 5 liters (10 pints) of body fluid during a race. Other studies report the loss of 500 to 1500ml (1 to 3 pints) of fluid per hour of exercise—and a level of just 2 percent dehydration hampers athletic performance. Dehydration also causes a rise in heart rate, increased "stickiness," or thickness, of the blood—causing raised blood pressure—and a far higher perception of effort.

Even if you have never felt a desire to drink while exercising, take the advice of the experts and try to consume more fluid. Start gradually, sipping water regularly, rather than gulping down large quantities at once, which may leave you feeling full and bloated. To offset the fluid loss resulting from exercise, give some thought to drinking before, during, and after your workout.

FLUID INTAKE GUIDELINES

The American College of Sports Medicine provides the following advice on fluid intake.
BEFORE EXERCISE Consume 300 to 500ml (up to 1 pint) of fluid 15–30 minutes before your workout. It doesn't have to be all in one swallow.
DURING EXERCISE Aim to drink 125ml to 250ml (up to half a pint) every 15 minutes. If you are exercising for an hour or more, isotonic sports drinks, containing electrolytes such as salt and potassium, as well as easily ingested carbohydrate and water, are more effective at delaying fatigue and enhancing performance than plain water.
AFTER EXERCISE After a tough session, you may want to rehydrate with a sports drink, or a carbohydrate-rich fluid such as fruit-flavored juice. Regardless of how long or intense your session was, you should drink at least 500ml (1 pint) of fluid afterward. If you exercised for an hour or more, aim for 1 liter (2 pints) and keep drinking regularly for the next few hours until your urine is the color of pale straw or lighter.

STAYING
MOTIVATED

MAINTAINING THE IMPETUS

Fitness is a journey rather than a destination. Depressing as it may seem, there will never be a time when you are "fit enough" to stop exercising. The important thing is to enjoy the journey, to make sure it is one that you will continue on for the rest of your life. That doesn't mean there won't be setbacks or periods when it all comes tumbling down—it's not easy to fit yet another task into a busy life—so be prepared to accept obstacles on the path to a fitter, healthier body.

Don't be too hard on yourself if you miss some of your fitness sessions. Instead, acknowledge that you have managed to do something, and build on that. Here are some other ways of getting—and keeping—the exercise habit.
Be organized and well prepared for exercise Keep a gym bag in the car or by your desk with clean kit inside for impromptu gym visits. Make sure your gear is washed and ready the day before you are going to exercise. Book courts, classes, and sessions in advance rather than leaving arrangements until the last minute.
Reward yourself for following your exercise program Perhaps a sports massage, a session with a personal trainer, or some new gear will maintain your enthusiasm.
Find other likeminded people to enjoy being active with Research shows that exercisers who train with others are less likely to drop out than those who do it alone.
Renew your goals regularly Having a purpose for every workout makes it all feel much more worthwhile. If you don't know why you are doing it, you will probably just "go through the motions," and you won't get much out of it. Have something to aim for.
Make changes Even if you love your Pilates classes or your running program, don't be afraid to shake things up now and then. Go try a sport you've never done before, take part in a race or charity event, or go to a different class, gym, or outdoor setting for a change of scene.
Focus on the process rather than the result Enjoy the feeling of moving your body to music, the sensation of being in water, or the renewed energy you get from yogic breathing, rather than worrying about fitness gains or weight loss.

> "'Tis a lesson you should heed, try, try again. If at first you don't succeed, try, try again."
> W.E. HICKSON (1803–70)

MOTIVATION OVERCOMING HURDLES

Let's face it, there are times when exercise seems more like a chore than a pleasure, when lounging on the sofa is far more appealing than getting your workout gear on. Don't be discouraged. The chances are, if you can just get yourself going, you will be really glad you did so. If you can't face your usual workout, pledge to do just half of it, and then see whether you want to carry on—or do the whole workout at a leisurely pace, rather than pushing yourself hard.

It is fine to skip the odd workout simply because you don't feel like it, but if you are missing scheduled sessions regularly, or you have dropped out altogether, it is worth examining the cause, and thinking about changes you could introduce to your regime to make it fun and enjoyable again.

The explanation for loss of motivation may be that you have simply lost sight of what you hoped to gain from being more active. However, it is possible that you have been overdoing things and are suffering from "burnout" or overtraining syndrome. Some of the symptoms of overtraining include fatigue, a weakened immune system, irritability, poor performance, guilt and worry about your workouts, and a raised resting heart rate (see page 14). If this is the case, then rest is the first line of defence. Put your goals aside temporarily and start exercising again only when your body and mind feel ready for it. If you feel too anxious or guilty to take time out, you may want to seek help from a doctor or psychotherapist. Don't become a slave to your fitness routine.

To discover the cause of your problem and decide how to put it right, re-read the section on goal-setting (see pages 28–29), then go through the motivational checklist below. You may also want to look at pages 41–48 to discover whether bad eating habits are undermining your efforts.

MOTIVATIONAL CHECKLIST

IS MY WORKOUT BORING? If so, think about ways to make it more interesting, or consider whether you need to try something new. Go back to chapter 2 (pages 17–30) to discover alternative ways to meet your fitness goals.

DO I FEEL LIKE A FAILURE IN MY SPORT/ACTIVITY? If so, no wonder you don't feel motivated to continue. Could you switch to a lower level of competition, take a break from competition, change gym/club, or find a coach or trainer to help you out? Remember, success isn't only about being "the best" or winning.

IS MY SCHEDULE TOO HEAVY? If you have bitten off more than you can chew, reassess your program and goals, and draw up something less daunting.

AM I GETTING RESULTS? A lack of progress can be very demotivating. Do you think your program is under-challenging, and therefore not yielding results? Or are you adhering to it so haphazardly that you haven't yet had a chance to see whether it works?

MORE PURPOSEFUL WORKOUTS

When you are working out, are you "switched on" to what is going on inside your body? If so, you are what is known as an "associator." "Disassociators" tend to "switch off" during exercise and aren't consciously aware of how they feel, the rhythm of their breathing, and so on—it's a bit like being on "autopilot." There are proponents for each style (you may want to disassociate during the last painful miles of a marathon, for example), but to make exercise more of a mind–body experience, try association.

As you begin your workout, concentrate on your breathing, tuning in to its rhythm. Be aware of your posture and how your limbs are moving, and think about how your heart is pumping faster to distribute blood to the working muscles. As your attention wanders, bring it back inside your body and picture your muscles getting stronger and firmer, your spine lengthening, your lungs filling with air. You will be surprised at how "connected" this technique can make you feel.

TAKE YOUR WORKOUTS OUTSIDE

Another way to get more meaning from your workout is to take it outside. We have so little contact with nature in our daily lives that exercising in the natural world can be a nurturing and energizing experience. Immersing ourselves in nature has a positive effect on mood, energy levels, and general well-being. So, whether it's weight training with dumbbells in the garden, biking, jogging, or hiking in the countryside, try an outdoor workout. Notice the breeze on your face, the smell of the flowers, the birds and butterflies, the feel of the grass under your feet—and feel good in the knowledge that you tend to burn more calories outside than in, because when you are outside you need to deal with the inconsistencies of the terrain, gradient, wind, and temperature.

TAKING A BREAK WHEN THE REST OF LIFE INTERVENES

There will be a time in your life when exercise has to take a back seat. Maybe you are working on a crucial project, studying for exams, getting married—and you just don't have time for your usual workouts.

All is not lost. Increasing the amount and intensity of "lifestyle activities" can help you maintain the fitness you have gained so far, and prevent unwanted weight gain. A study by the Cooper Institute in Dallas, Texas, found that lifestyle activities such as stair climbing and parking your car far away from the stores could have similar benefits to working out at a gym. The same researchers estimated that modern adults burn 300 to 700 fewer calories per day than their ancestors simply because they expend less energy on daily tasks. So look for opportunities to be more active in your daily life. For example, use a basket instead of a cart to carry lighter loads at the supermarket, or put music on while you do tasks such as sorting laundry to encourage you to move your body. Take things upstairs when you need to rather than leaving a pile of items to take up all at once. Every extra step counts!

It is a good idea to reduce your daily calorie intake slightly when you are using less energy—see pages 41–48 for advice on healthy eating and weight control.

EIGHT WAYS TO BURN 150 CALORIES WITHOUT GOING NEAR THE GYM!

clean your own windows for 45 minutes	= 150 calories
wash the car for 45–60 minutes	= 150 calories
wash windows or floors for 45–60 minutes	= 150 calories
work in the garden for 30–45 minutes	= 150 calories
push a stroller for 30 minutes	= 150 calories
rake leaves for 30 minutes	= 150 calories
walk at 15-minute-mile pace for 30 minutes	= 150 calories
climb stairs for 15 minutes	= 150 calories

MY JOURNAL

MY JOURNAL

KEEPING A FITNESS JOURNAL

As you will have realized by now, *My Fitness Journal* is more than a book. The best way to see it is as a tool to help you get and stay fit, make sure you are doing it right, and monitor your progress. In this section, there is plenty of space to record your fitness highs and lows, your goals and aspirations.

Research shows that keeping a training log acts as a powerful motivator to both new and existing exercisers. It is also useful in a more practical way: if you develop an injury, or feel your fitness is not improving, you can look back and see what you have been doing, and search for clues to why the event has occurred.

Fill in as much or as little as you wish on each of the weekly diary pages. You may simply want to record the fact that you went for a half-hour bicycle ride, but if you are in a more expansive mood, there is space to write down how far you went, what the weather was like, how difficult the session felt, how it affected your mood, and so on.

At the end of each six-week segment of the journal, you will find a Taking Stock page consisting of several questions relating to your fitness program. This is designed to give you the opportunity to refocus—rather than simply soldiering on, uncertain whether you are headed where you want to go. As you consider your answers to the questions in Taking Stock, look back over the previous six weeks' journal entries, and if you feel like it, repeat some of the tests described on pages 14–16. To measure your long-term progress, record your results on the pull-out Fitness Chart contained in the pocket at the front of this section.

Along with Taking Stock, you will also find a Food Diary to fill in. Use it to record everything you eat and drink on a typical day and compare this with the healthy eating checklist that appears on the reverse side of the Fitness Chart.

A word of warning: keeping a fitness journal is addictive! Stick with it for a few days, and before you know it you will find that it becomes as much a part of your routine as the workouts themselves.

> "Every journey begins with a single step."
> CONFUCIUS

WEEK	TYPE OF ACTIVITY	LENGTH OF TIME OR DISTANCE	DETAILS
MONDAY date			
TUESDAY date			
WEDNESDAY date			
THURSDAY date			
FRIDAY date			
SATURDAY date			
SUNDAY date			

My week:

HOW THE WORKOUT FELT	MY MOOD BEFORE, DURING, AND AFTER	OTHER COMMENTS

WEEK	TYPE OF ACTIVITY	LENGTH OF TIME OR DISTANCE	DETAILS
MONDAY date			
TUESDAY date			
WEDNESDAY date			
THURSDAY date			
FRIDAY date			
SATURDAY date			
SUNDAY date			

THE PAYOFFS OF PERFECT POSTURE Standing correctly reduces stress on the spinal structures and works the abdominal muscles all day long. Good posture also conveys confidence, and cuts incidence of back pain, headaches, and neck strain. It prevents muscle imbalances such as tight chest muscles and weak shoulder girdle muscles. And it opens the chest, using more of lung capacity for breathing.

HOW THE WORKOUT FELT	MY MOOD BEFORE, DURING, AND AFTER	OTHER COMMENTS

My week:

WEEK _____	TYPE OF ACTIVITY	LENGTH OF TIME OR DISTANCE	DETAILS
MONDAY date _____			
TUESDAY date _____			
WEDNESDAY date _____			
THURSDAY date _____			
FRIDAY date _____			
SATURDAY date _____			
SUNDAY date _____			

My week: _____

_____

_____

_____

HOW THE WORKOUT FELT	MY MOOD BEFORE, DURING, AND AFTER	OTHER COMMENTS

WEEK	TYPE OF ACTIVITY	LENGTH OF TIME OR DISTANCE	DETAILS
MONDAY date			
TUESDAY date			
WEDNESDAY date			
THURSDAY date			
FRIDAY date			
SATURDAY date			
SUNDAY date			

My week:

HOW THE WORKOUT FELT	MY MOOD BEFORE, DURING, AND AFTER	OTHER COMMENTS

WEEK	TYPE OF ACTIVITY	LENGTH OF TIME OR DISTANCE	DETAILS
MONDAY date			
TUESDAY date			
WEDNESDAY date			
THURSDAY date			
FRIDAY date			
SATURDAY date			
SUNDAY date			

My week:

HOW THE WORKOUT FELT	MY MOOD BEFORE, DURING, AND AFTER	OTHER COMMENTS

STAYING COOL IN THE HEAT If you are exercising outdoors in hot weather, remember your sunblock. You may not be lying on the beach, but doesn't mean you're not getting burned. Use a high protection factor designed specially for sport so it won't sweat off in the first few minutes. Protect your eyes from the sun's rays with sunglasses. Drink plenty of fluid to avoid getting dehydrated in the heat.

WEEK	TYPE OF ACTIVITY	LENGTH OF TIME OR DISTANCE	DETAILS
MONDAY date			
TUESDAY date			
WEDNESDAY date			
THURSDAY date			
FRIDAY date			
SATURDAY date			
SUNDAY date			

My week:

HOW THE WORKOUT FELT	MY MOOD BEFORE, DURING, AND AFTER	OTHER COMMENTS

TODAY'S DATE _____

TAKING STOCK OF YOUR PROGRESS

Congratulations on your efforts during the past six weeks of regular exercise. It is now time to review your progress. Answer the questions below and fill out the food diary—remember to compare your intake with the healthy eating guidelines on the pull-out card.

Have I followed my program over the last six weeks? _____

Have I reached my goals or am I closer to them? _____

What was particularly good or bad about my program?

_____

_____

What changes can I make to enhance improvements over the next six weeks?

_____

_____

FOOD DIARY FOR A TYPICAL DAY

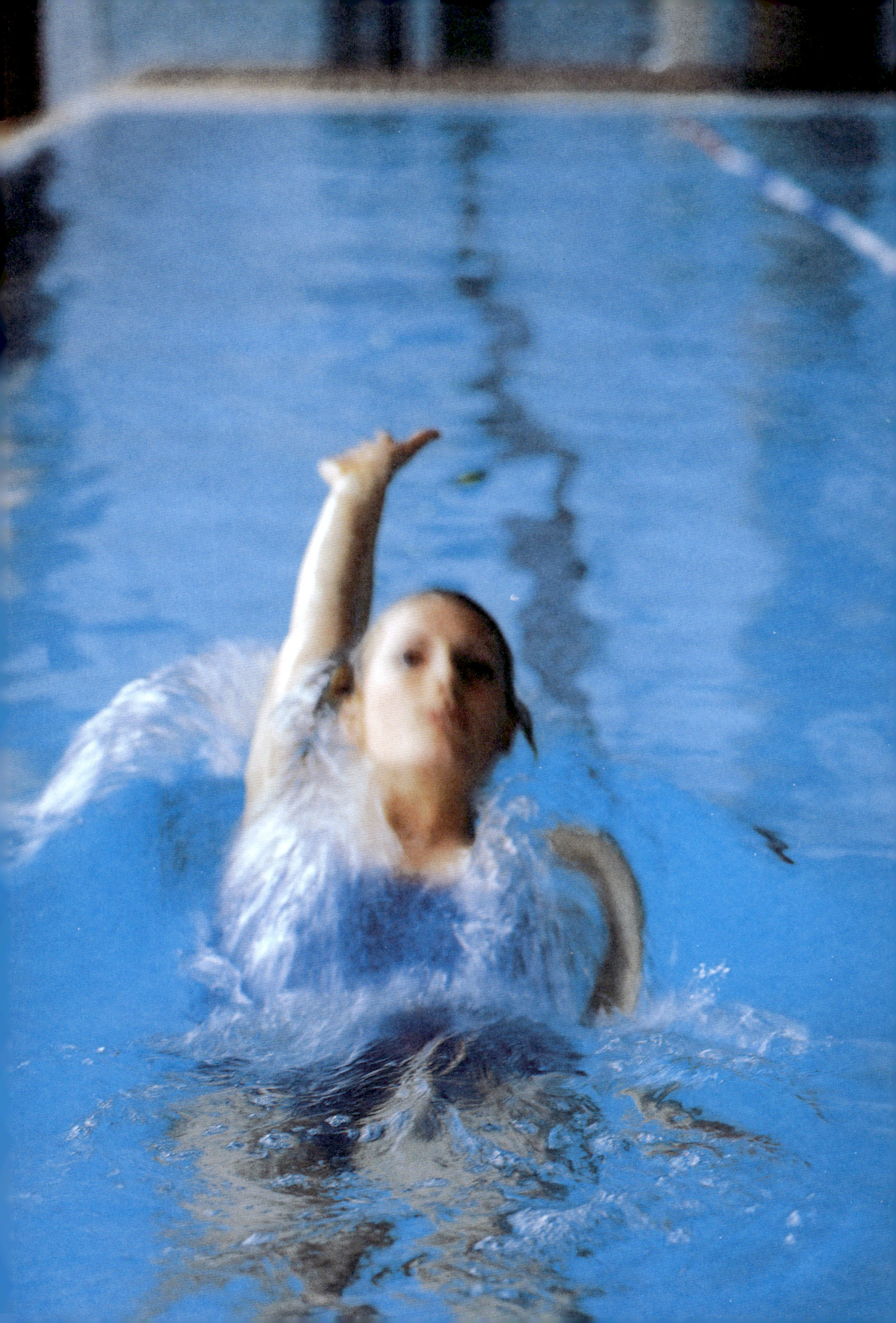

WEEK	TYPE OF ACTIVITY	LENGTH OF TIME OR DISTANCE	DETAILS
MONDAY date			
TUESDAY date			
WEDNESDAY date			
THURSDAY date			
FRIDAY date			
SATURDAY date			
SUNDAY date			

My week:

HOW THE WORKOUT FELT	MY MOOD BEFORE, DURING, AND AFTER	OTHER COMMENTS

WEEK _____	TYPE OF ACTIVITY	LENGTH OF TIME OR DISTANCE	DETAILS
MONDAY date _____			
TUESDAY date _____			
WEDNESDAY date _____			
THURSDAY date _____			
FRIDAY date _____			
SATURDAY date _____			
SUNDAY date _____			

DEALING WITH INJURIES

If you sustain a muscular or other soft tissue injury during your workout, give it the RICE treatment: rest, ice, compression, and elevation. This will help minimize swelling and inflammation in the injured area. If RICE does not alleviate the problem, visit a sport injury clinic, physiotherapist, or doctor as soon as you can.

HOW THE WORKOUT FELT	MY MOOD BEFORE, DURING, AND AFTER	OTHER COMMENTS

My week:

WEEK	TYPE OF ACTIVITY	LENGTH OF TIME OR DISTANCE	DETAILS
MONDAY date			
TUESDAY date			
WEDNESDAY date			
THURSDAY date			
FRIDAY date			
SATURDAY date			
SUNDAY date			

My week: _____
_____
_____
_____

HOW THE WORKOUT FELT	MY MOOD BEFORE, DURING, AND AFTER	OTHER COMMENTS

WEEK _____	TYPE OF ACTIVITY	LENGTH OF TIME OR DISTANCE	DETAILS
MONDAY date _____			
TUESDAY date _____			
WEDNESDAY date _____			
THURSDAY date _____			
FRIDAY date _____			
SATURDAY date _____			
SUNDAY date _____			

My week: _____
_____
_____
_____

HOW THE WORKOUT FELT	MY MOOD BEFORE, DURING, AND AFTER	OTHER COMMENTS

WEEK	TYPE OF ACTIVITY	LENGTH OF TIME OR DISTANCE	DETAILS
MONDAY date			
TUESDAY date			
WEDNESDAY date			
THURSDAY date			
FRIDAY date			
SATURDAY date			
SUNDAY date			

My week:

HOW THE WORKOUT FELT	MY MOOD BEFORE, DURING, AND AFTER	OTHER COMMENTS

HOME GYM EQUIPMENT

A good-quality exercise mat is advisable for floor exercise, to protect your spine and provide a nonslip surface. Resistance bands or tubes take up little space and save the cost of a range of dumbbells of different weights. A fit ball (an oversized inflatable ball to challenge stability and provide resistance) is a great buy for abdominal, back, and bottom exercises.

WEEK	TYPE OF ACTIVITY	LENGTH OF TIME OR DISTANCE	DETAILS
MONDAY date			
TUESDAY date			
WEDNESDAY date			
THURSDAY date			
FRIDAY date			
SATURDAY date			
SUNDAY date			

My week:

HOW THE WORKOUT FELT	MY MOOD BEFORE, DURING, AND AFTER	OTHER COMMENTS

TODAY'S DATE _____

TAKING STOCK OF YOUR PROGRESS

Congratulations on your efforts during the past six weeks of regular exercise. It is now time to review your progress. Answer the questions below and fill out the food diary—remember to compare your intake with the healthy eating guidelines on the pull-out card.

Have I followed my program over the last six weeks? _____

Have I reached my goals or am I closer to them? _____

What was particularly good or bad about my program?

_____

_____

What changes can I make to enhance improvements over the next six weeks?

_____

_____

FOOD DIARY FOR A TYPICAL DAY

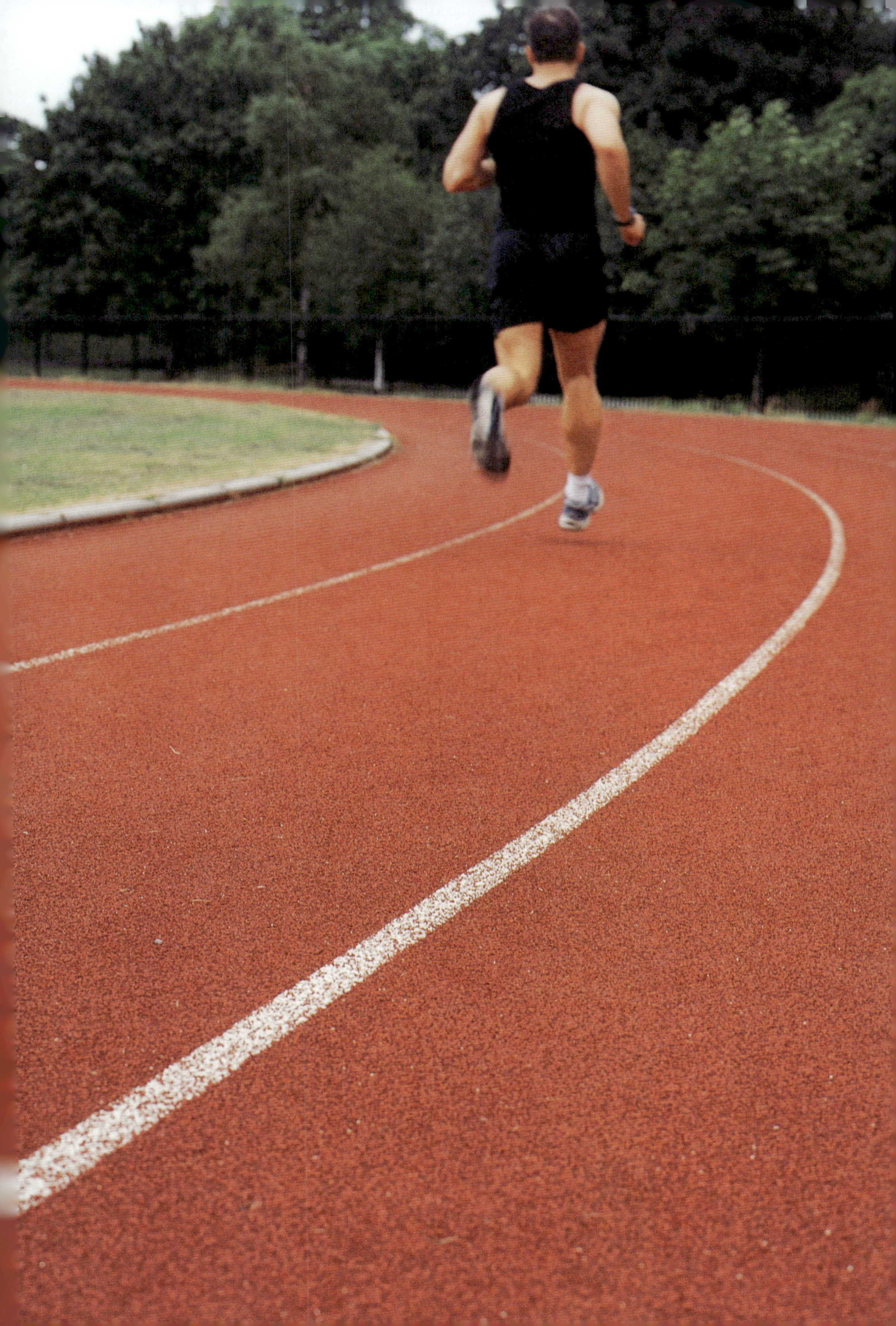

WEEK	TYPE OF ACTIVITY	LENGTH OF TIME OR DISTANCE	DETAILS
MONDAY date			
TUESDAY date			
WEDNESDAY date			
THURSDAY date			
FRIDAY date			
SATURDAY date			
SUNDAY date			

My week:

HOW THE WORKOUT FELT	MY MOOD BEFORE, DURING, AND AFTER	OTHER COMMENTS

WEEK	TYPE OF ACTIVITY	LENGTH OF TIME OR DISTANCE	DETAILS
MONDAY date			
TUESDAY date			
WEDNESDAY date			
THURSDAY date			
FRIDAY date			
SATURDAY date			
SUNDAY date			

WEAR THE RIGHT SHOES

Buy the right shoes for your sport. Cross-trainers are only suitable if you do a variety of activities with only a little high-impact exercise. Visit a specialist store where you can get advice on the right type of shoe to suit your foot, your "gait" (the way you walk), and your activity. Go in the afternoon, when your feet will be a little larger, and wear sports socks.

HOW THE WORKOUT FELT	MY MOOD BEFORE, DURING, AND AFTER	OTHER COMMENTS

My week: _____
_____
_____
_____

WEEK	TYPE OF ACTIVITY	LENGTH OF TIME OR DISTANCE	DETAILS
MONDAY date _____			
TUESDAY date _____			
WEDNESDAY date _____			
THURSDAY date _____			
FRIDAY date _____			
SATURDAY date _____			
SUNDAY date _____			

My week: _____

HOW THE WORKOUT FELT	MY MOOD BEFORE, DURING, AND AFTER	OTHER COMMENTS

WEEK	TYPE OF ACTIVITY	LENGTH OF TIME OR DISTANCE	DETAILS
MONDAY date			
TUESDAY date			
WEDNESDAY date			
THURSDAY date			
FRIDAY date			
SATURDAY date			
SUNDAY date			

My week:

HOW THE WORKOUT FELT	MY MOOD BEFORE, DURING, AND AFTER	OTHER COMMENTS

WEEK	TYPE OF ACTIVITY	LENGTH OF TIME OR DISTANCE	DETAILS
MONDAY date			
TUESDAY date			
WEDNESDAY date			
THURSDAY date			
FRIDAY date			
SATURDAY date			
SUNDAY date			

My week: _____

HOW THE WORKOUT FELT	MY MOOD BEFORE, DURING, AND AFTER	OTHER COMMENTS

STEPPING UP THE BURN Want to increase your fat-burning potential without making time for longer workouts? Introduce short bursts of high-intensity activity into your usual aerobic workout. For example, instead of jogging for 20 minutes, jog for 5 to warm up, then run fast for 2 minutes, recover at a jogging pace for 3 minutes—repeat 3 times. Try it with swimming, cycling, skating, walking.

WEEK ____	TYPE OF ACTIVITY	LENGTH OF TIME OR DISTANCE	DETAILS
MONDAY date ____			
TUESDAY date ____			
WEDNESDAY date ____			
THURSDAY date ____			
FRIDAY date ____			
SATURDAY date ____			
SUNDAY date ____			

My week: _____

HOW THE WORKOUT FELT	MY MOOD BEFORE, DURING, AND AFTER	OTHER COMMENTS

TODAY'S DATE _____

TAKING STOCK OF YOUR PROGRESS

Congratulations on your efforts during the past six weeks of regular exercise. It is now time to review your progress. Answer the questions below and fill out the food diary—remember to compare your intake with the healthy eating guidelines on the pull-out card.

Have I followed my program over the last six weeks? _____

Have I reached my goals or am I closer to them? _____

What was particularly good or bad about my program?

_____

_____

What changes can I make to enhance improvements over the next six weeks?

_____

_____

FOOD DIARY FOR A TYPICAL DAY

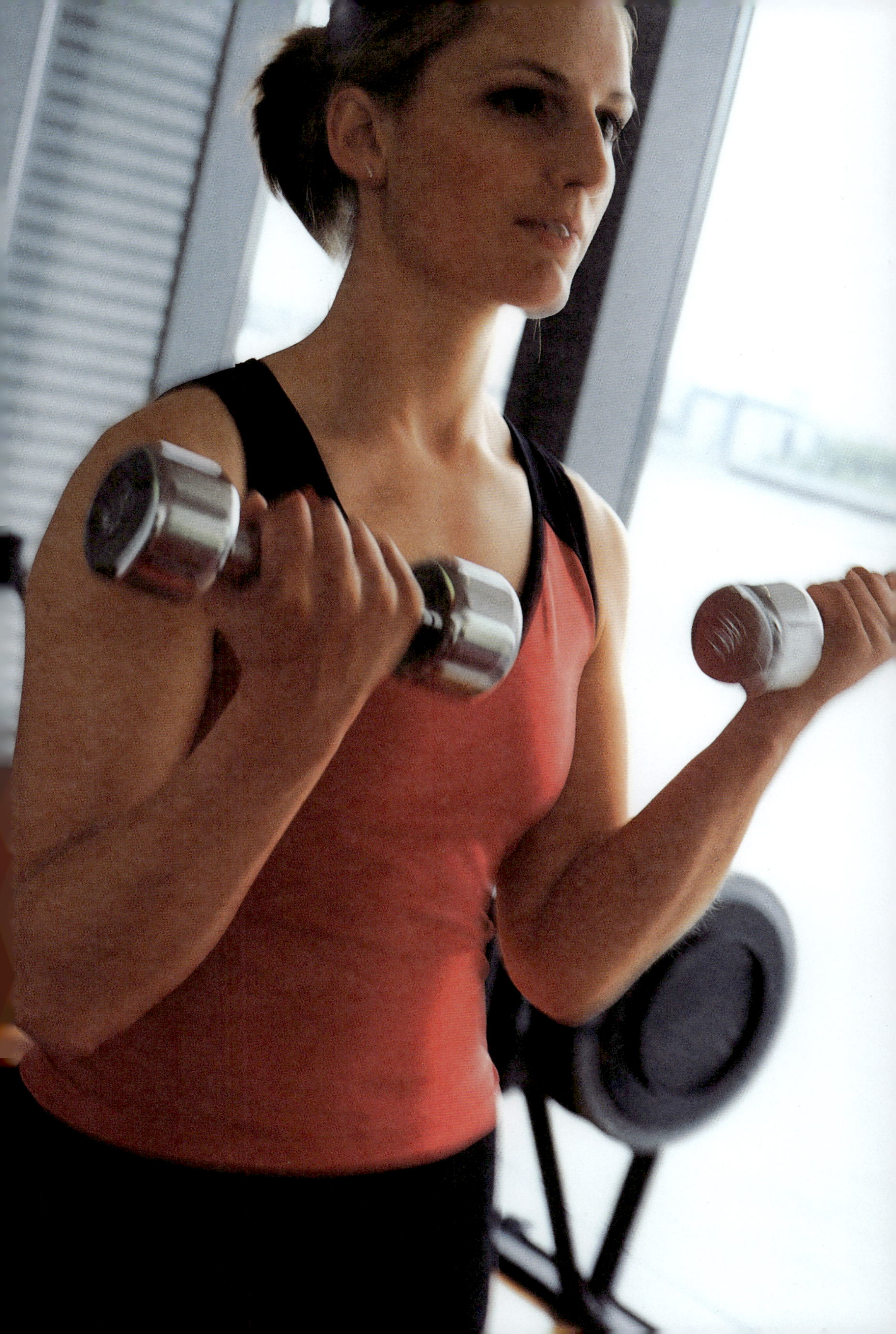

WEEK	TYPE OF ACTIVITY	LENGTH OF TIME OR DISTANCE	DETAILS
MONDAY date			
TUESDAY date			
WEDNESDAY date			
THURSDAY date			
FRIDAY date			
SATURDAY date			
SUNDAY date			

My week:

HOW THE WORKOUT FELT	MY MOOD BEFORE, DURING, AND AFTER	OTHER COMMENTS

WEEK _____	TYPE OF ACTIVITY	LENGTH OF TIME OR DISTANCE	DETAILS
MONDAY date _____			
TUESDAY date _____			
WEDNESDAY date _____			
THURSDAY date _____			
FRIDAY date _____			
SATURDAY date _____			
SUNDAY date _____			

WORKING OUT IN WINTER

If you are exercising outdoors in winter, dress in layers so that you can peel them off as your body warms up. One thick heavy garment will soon get sweaty and too warm. Protect your extremities with gloves and a hat, and wear or carry a waterproof jacket. Make sure you wear something reflective on dark mornings and evenings so you can easily be seen.

HOW THE WORKOUT FELT	MY MOOD BEFORE, DURING, AND AFTER	OTHER COMMENTS

My week:

WEEK ____	TYPE OF ACTIVITY	LENGTH OF TIME OR DISTANCE	DETAILS
MONDAY date ____			
TUESDAY date ____			
WEDNESDAY date ____			
THURSDAY date ____			
FRIDAY date ____			
SATURDAY date ____			
SUNDAY date ____			

My week: _____

HOW THE WORKOUT FELT	MY MOOD BEFORE, DURING, AND AFTER	OTHER COMMENTS

WEEK	TYPE OF ACTIVITY	LENGTH OF TIME OR DISTANCE	DETAILS
MONDAY date			
TUESDAY date			
WEDNESDAY date			
THURSDAY date			
FRIDAY date			
SATURDAY date			
SUNDAY date			

My week:

HOW THE WORKOUT FELT	MY MOOD BEFORE, DURING, AND AFTER	OTHER COMMENTS

WEEK _____	TYPE OF ACTIVITY	LENGTH OF TIME OR DISTANCE	DETAILS
MONDAY date _____			
TUESDAY date _____			
WEDNESDAY date _____			
THURSDAY date _____			
FRIDAY date _____			
SATURDAY date _____			
SUNDAY date _____			

My week: _____

HOW THE WORKOUT FELT	MY MOOD BEFORE, DURING, AND AFTER	OTHER COMMENTS

A WOMAN'S BEST FRIEND

One of the most important items of clothing for any active woman is a sports bra—but only 35 percent of female exercisers wear a proper sports bra, research reveals. Over time, lack of a good bra causes the ligaments supporting the breasts to sag irreversibly. Even if you are an A-cup, your breasts move about 1½ in (40mm) during exercise without a bra.

WEEK	TYPE OF ACTIVITY	LENGTH OF TIME OR DISTANCE	DETAILS
MONDAY date _____			
TUESDAY date _____			
WEDNESDAY date _____			
THURSDAY date _____			
FRIDAY date _____			
SATURDAY date _____			
SUNDAY date _____			

My week: _____

_____

_____

_____

HOW THE WORKOUT FELT	MY MOOD BEFORE, DURING, AND AFTER	OTHER COMMENTS

TODAY'S DATE _____

TAKING STOCK OF YOUR PROGRESS

Congratulations on your efforts during the past six weeks of regular exercise. It is now time to review your progress. Answer the questions below and fill out the food diary—remember to compare your intake with the healthy eating guidelines on the pull-out card.

Have I followed my program over the last six weeks? _____

Have I reached my goals or am I closer to them? _____

What was particularly good or bad about my program?

_____

_____

What changes can I make to enhance improvements over the next six weeks?

_____

_____

FOOD DIARY FOR A TYPICAL DAY

_____
_____
_____
_____
_____
_____
_____
_____
_____
_____
_____
_____
_____
_____

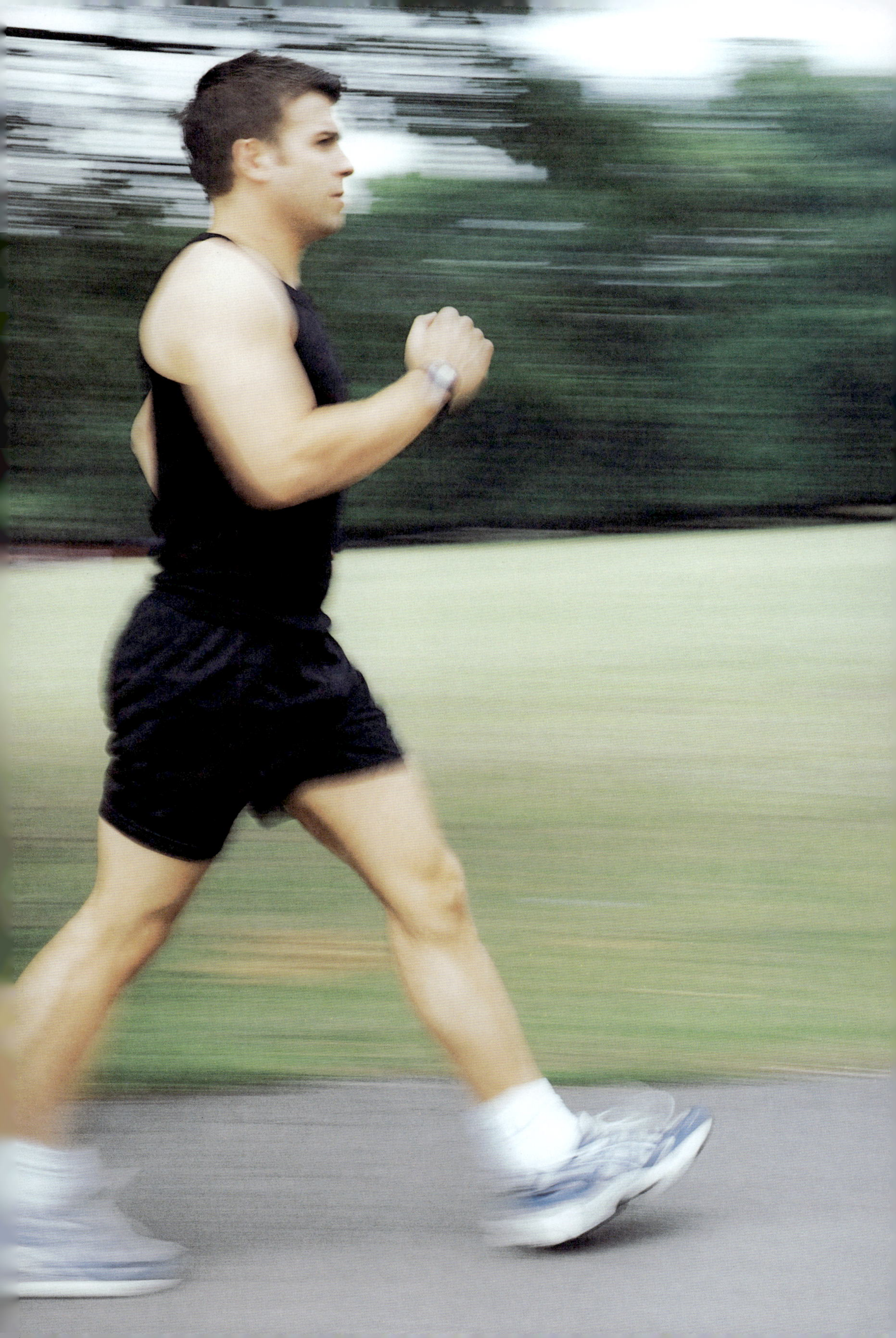

WEEK	TYPE OF ACTIVITY	LENGTH OF TIME OR DISTANCE	DETAILS
MONDAY date			
TUESDAY date			
WEDNESDAY date			
THURSDAY date			
FRIDAY date			
SATURDAY date			
SUNDAY date			

My week:

HOW THE WORKOUT FELT	MY MOOD BEFORE, DURING, AND AFTER	OTHER COMMENTS

WEEK _____	TYPE OF ACTIVITY	LENGTH OF TIME OR DISTANCE	DETAILS
MONDAY date _____			
TUESDAY date _____			
WEDNESDAY date _____			
THURSDAY date _____			
FRIDAY date _____			
SATURDAY date _____			
SUNDAY date _____			

WORKOUT WINDOWS No time for a full-blown workout? Researchers at the University of Ulster in Northern Ireland found that brisk 10-minute blocks were as effective as more prolonged efforts in boosting aerobic fitness and cholesterol profile, and alleviating anxiety and stress. Accumulating 30 minutes a day in 10-minute bursts will improve heart health and cardiovascular fitness.

HOW THE WORKOUT FELT	MY MOOD BEFORE, DURING, AND AFTER	OTHER COMMENTS

My week: _____
_____
_____
_____

WEEK	TYPE OF ACTIVITY	LENGTH OF TIME OR DISTANCE	DETAILS
MONDAY date			
TUESDAY date			
WEDNESDAY date			
THURSDAY date			
FRIDAY date			
SATURDAY date			
SUNDAY date			

My week:

HOW THE WORKOUT FELT	MY MOOD BEFORE, DURING, AND AFTER	OTHER COMMENTS

WEEK	TYPE OF ACTIVITY	LENGTH OF TIME OR DISTANCE	DETAILS
MONDAY date			
TUESDAY date			
WEDNESDAY date			
THURSDAY date			
FRIDAY date			
SATURDAY date			
SUNDAY date			

My week: _____
_____
_____
_____

HOW THE WORKOUT FELT	MY MOOD BEFORE, DURING, AND AFTER	OTHER COMMENTS

WEEK	TYPE OF ACTIVITY	LENGTH OF TIME OR DISTANCE	DETAILS
MONDAY date			
TUESDAY date			
WEDNESDAY date			
THURSDAY date			
FRIDAY date			
SATURDAY date			
SUNDAY date			

My week:

HOW THE WORKOUT FELT	MY MOOD BEFORE, DURING, AND AFTER	OTHER COMMENTS

HIDDEN CALORIES — If you are eating healthily and exercising regularly but not shedding body fat, liquid calories, particularly those in alcoholic drinks, could be to blame. A glass of wine (5fl.oz./140ml) contains 100 calories, while a pint of beer contains 170 calories. And once you have had a couple of drinks, you are more likely to overindulge in nuts, potato chips, and other snacks.

WEEK	TYPE OF ACTIVITY	LENGTH OF TIME OR DISTANCE	DETAILS
MONDAY date			
TUESDAY date			
WEDNESDAY date			
THURSDAY date			
FRIDAY date			
SATURDAY date			
SUNDAY date			

My week:

HOW THE WORKOUT FELT	MY MOOD BEFORE, DURING, AND AFTER	OTHER COMMENTS

TODAY'S DATE _____

TAKING STOCK OF YOUR PROGRESS

Congratulations on your efforts during the past six weeks of regular exercise. It is now time to review your progress. Answer the questions below and fill out the food diary—remember to compare your intake with the healthy eating guidelines on the pull-out card.

Have I followed my program over the last six weeks? _____

Have I reached my goals or am I closer to them? _____

What was particularly good or bad about my program?

_____

_____

What changes can I make to enhance improvements over the next six weeks?

_____

_____

FOOD DIARY FOR A TYPICAL DAY

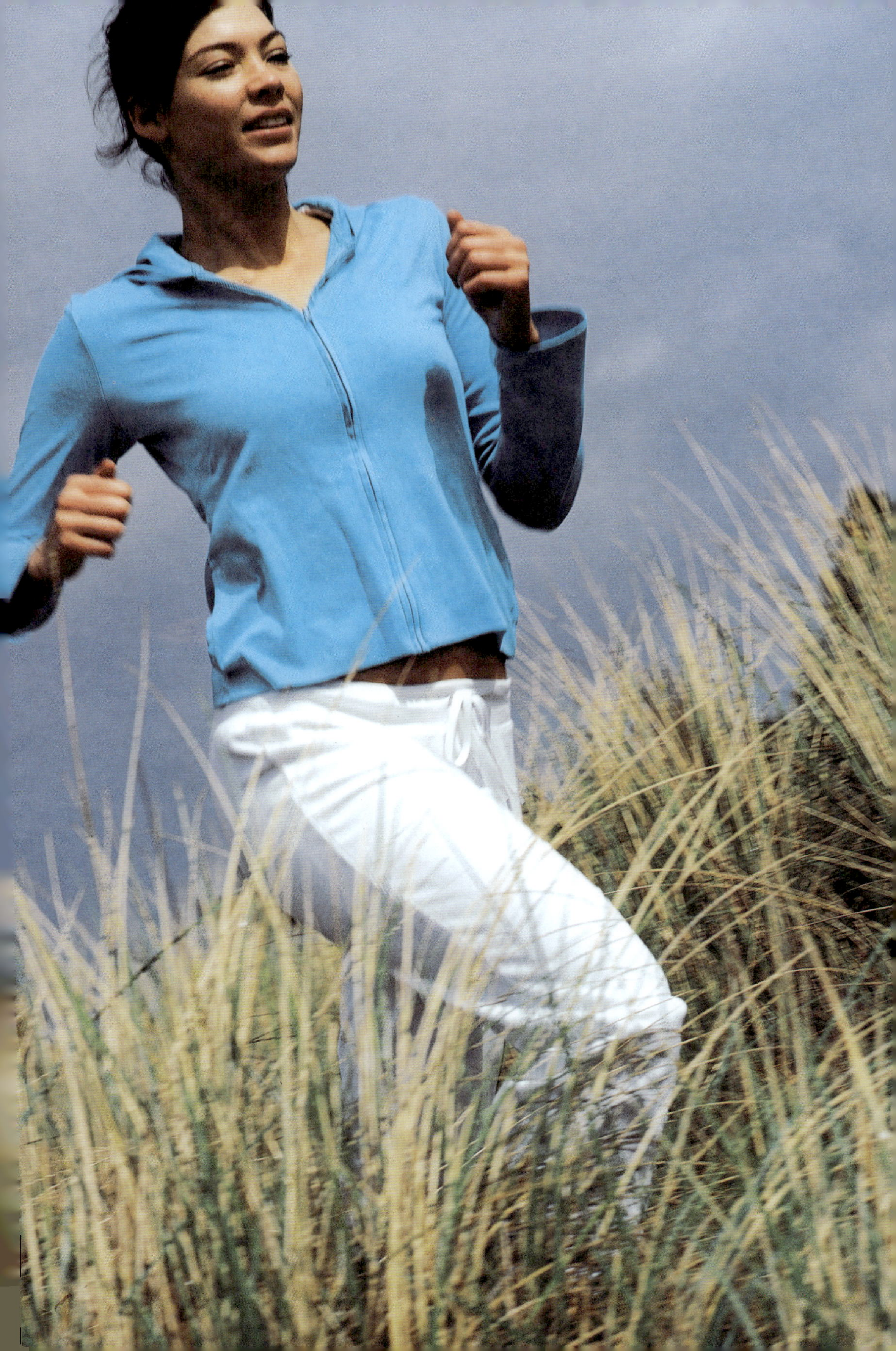

WEEK _____	TYPE OF ACTIVITY	LENGTH OF TIME OR DISTANCE	DETAILS
MONDAY date _____			
TUESDAY date _____			
WEDNESDAY date _____			
THURSDAY date _____			
FRIDAY date _____			
SATURDAY date _____			
SUNDAY date _____			

My week: _____

HOW THE WORKOUT FELT	MY MOOD BEFORE, DURING, AND AFTER	OTHER COMMENTS

WEEK	TYPE OF ACTIVITY	LENGTH OF TIME OR DISTANCE	DETAILS
MONDAY date			
TUESDAY date			
WEDNESDAY date			
THURSDAY date			
FRIDAY date			
SATURDAY date			
SUNDAY date			

LARKS AND OWLS

Early-morning workouts can set you up for the day, but they don't suit everyone. A study in the *British Journal of Sports Medicine* found that early exercise can have a detrimental effect on the immune system. If you prefer to leave your workout until later in the day, then do so—it is better to follow your natural diurnal rhythms than force yourself to be active.

HOW THE WORKOUT FELT	MY MOOD BEFORE, DURING, AND AFTER	OTHER COMMENTS

My week: _____
_____
_____
_____

WEEK	TYPE OF ACTIVITY	LENGTH OF TIME OR DISTANCE	DETAILS
MONDAY date			
TUESDAY date			
WEDNESDAY date			
THURSDAY date			
FRIDAY date			
SATURDAY date			
SUNDAY date			

My week:

HOW THE WORKOUT FELT	MY MOOD BEFORE, DURING, AND AFTER	OTHER COMMENTS

WEEK	TYPE OF ACTIVITY	LENGTH OF TIME OR DISTANCE	DETAILS
MONDAY date			
TUESDAY date			
WEDNESDAY date			
THURSDAY date			
FRIDAY date			
SATURDAY date			
SUNDAY date			

My week:

HOW THE WORKOUT FELT	MY MOOD BEFORE, DURING, AND AFTER	OTHER COMMENTS

WEEK _____	TYPE OF ACTIVITY	LENGTH OF TIME OR DISTANCE	DETAILS
MONDAY date _____			
TUESDAY date _____			
WEDNESDAY date _____			
THURSDAY date _____			
FRIDAY date _____			
SATURDAY date _____			
SUNDAY date _____			

My week: _____

_____

_____

_____

HOW THE WORKOUT FELT	MY MOOD BEFORE, DURING, AND AFTER	OTHER COMMENTS

KEEPING UP THE PACE

You know that brisk walking counts as a bona fide workout, but what exactly is brisk? To reap tangible health and fitness benefits, you should walk 4 to 4.3 miles an hour, which equates to approximately 90–120 steps per minute. It should feel moderately challenging, but not uncomfortable. If you don't get out of breath, increase the pace a little to make it count.

WEEK _____	TYPE OF ACTIVITY	LENGTH OF TIME OR DISTANCE	DETAILS
MONDAY date _____			
TUESDAY date _____			
WEDNESDAY date _____			
THURSDAY date _____			
FRIDAY date _____			
SATURDAY date _____			
SUNDAY date _____			

My week: _____

_____

_____

_____

HOW THE WORKOUT FELT	MY MOOD BEFORE, DURING, AND AFTER	OTHER COMMENTS

TODAY'S DATE _____

TAKING STOCK OF YOUR PROGRESS

Congratulations on your efforts during the past six weeks of regular exercise. It is now time to review your progress. Answer the questions below and fill out the food diary—remember to compare your intake with the healthy eating guidelines on the pull-out card.

Have I followed my program over the last six weeks? _____

Have I reached my goals or am I closer to them? _____

What was particularly good or bad about my program?

_____

_____

What changes can I make to enhance improvements over the next six weeks?

_____

_____

FOOD DIARY FOR A TYPICAL DAY

RESOURCES

GENERAL FITNESS INFORMATION

American Council on Exercise
4851 Paramount Drive
San Diego, CA 92123, USA
+1 858 279 8227
www.acefitness.org
Works to improve professional standards in the fitness industry and encourage people of all ages to enjoy the benefits of exercise. Certifies fitness professionals in the USA and 77 other countries.

The Cooper Institute
12330 Preston Road
Dallas, TX 75230, USA
+1 972 341 3200
www.cooperinst.org
Promotes healthy living and certifies fitness professionals. Cooper Aerobics Institute runs fitness, weight loss, and stress management programs.

Fitness Industry Association
115 Eastbourne Mews
London W2 6LQ, UK
+44 (0)20 7298 6730
www.fia.org.uk
Promotes best practice in the health and fitness industry and sets performance standards for member clubs.

IDEA
6190 Cornerstone Court East
Suite 204
San Diego, CA 92121, USA
www.ideafit.com
A worldwide fitness association with more than 19,000 members in over 80 countries.

International Sports Sciences Association (ISSA)
400 E. Gutierrez Street
Santa Barbara, CA 93101, USA
+1 805 884 8111
www.issaonline.com
A leader in health and fitness certification.

Melpomene Institute
+1 651 642 1951
www.melpomene.org
Research and resource center for women interested in physical activity at all levels of frequency and intensity. Named for a Greek woman who ran the Olympic marathon in 1896.

National Athletic Trainers' Association
2952 Stemmons Freeway
Dallas, TX 75247, USA
+1 214 637 6282
www.nata.org

National Register of Personal Trainers
16 Borough High Street
London SE1 9QG, UK
+44 (0)870 200 6010
www.nrpt.org.uk

www.bbc.co.uk/health
BBC website with news and information on all aspects of health and healthy living; includes online courses.

SPORTS GOVERNING BODIES AND ASSOCIATIONS

British Orienteering Federation
Riversdale, Dale Road North
Darley Dale, Matlock
Derbyshire DE4 2HX, UK
+44 (0)1629 734042
www.britishorienteering.org.uk

British Surfing Association
The International Surfing Centre
Fistral Beach, Newquay
Cornwall TR7 1HY, UK
+44 (0)1637 876474
www.britsurf.co.uk

British Triathlon Association
P.O. Box 25, Loughborough
Leicestershire LE11 3WX, UK
+44 (0)1509 226161
www.britishtriathlon.org

Lawn Tennis Association
Palliser Road
London W14 9EG, UK
+44 (0)20 7381 7000
www.lta.org.uk

Trail Running Association
28 Radstock Lane
Earley
Reading
Berkshire RG6 5QL, UK
+44 (0)118 987 2736
www.tra-uk.org

United States Tennis Association
70 West Red Oak Lane
White Plains, New York 10604
USA
+1 914 696 7000
www.usta.com

USA Cycling
1 Olympic Plaza
Colorado Springs, CO 80909
USA
+1 719 866 4581
www.usacycling.org

USA Track & Field
One RCA Dome, Suite 140
Indianapolis, IN 46225, USA
+1 317 261 0500
www.usataf.org

USA Triathlon
616 W. Monument Street
Colorado Springs, CO 80905
USA
+1 719 597 9090
www.usatriathlon.org

Women's Running Network
59 Farm Hill, Exwick
Devon EX4 2LW, UK
+44 (0)1392 683318
www.womensrunningnetwork.co.uk
Aims to encourage and support new female runners.

www.british-athletics.co.uk
Directory of British Athletics clubs.

SPORTS NUTRITION AND SUPPLEMENTS

American College of Nutrition
300 S. Duncan Ave.
Ste. 225
Clearwater, FL 33755, USA
+1 727 446 6086
www.am-coll-nutr.org

British Nutrition Foundation
High Holborn House
52–54 High Holborn
London WC1V 6RQ
+44 (0)20 7404 6504
www.nutrition.org.uk

Gatorade Sports Science Institute
617 West Main Street
Barrington, Illinois 60010, USA
+1 800 616 4774
www.gssiweb.com

Higher Nature
The Nutrition Centre
Burwash Common
East Sussex TN19 7LX, UK
+44 (0)1435 884668
www.higher-nature.co.uk

The Nutri Centre
7 Park Crescent
London W1B 1PF, UK
+44 (0)20 7436 5122
www.nutricentre.com

Science in Sport
Ashwood Laboratories
Brockhall Village, Blackburn
Lancashire BB6 8BB, UK
+44 (0)1254 246061
www.scienceinsport.com

SPORTS INJURY PREVENTION AND TREATMENT

American College of Sports Medicine
P.O. Box 1440
Indianapolis, IN 46206, USA
+1 317 637 9200
www.acsm.com

American Orthopaedic Society for Sports Medicine
6300 N. River Road
Suite 500
Rosemont, IL 60018, USA
+1 847 292 4900
www.sportsmed.org

American Physical Therapy Association
1111 North Fairfax Street
Alexandria, VA 22314, USA
+1 703 684 2782
www.apta.org

Chartered Society of Physiotherapists
14 Bedford Row
London WC1R 4ED, UK
+44 (0)20 7306 6666
www.csp.org.uk

Crystal Palace National Sports
Centre Sports Injury Clinic
P.O. Box 676, Upper Norwood
London SE19 2BL, UK
+44 (0)20 8778 0131
www.crystalpalace.co.uk

Lilleshall National Sports Centre
Nr Newport
Shropshire TF10 9AT, UK
+44 (0)1952 603003
www.lilleshall.co.uk

Nicholas Institute of Sports Medicine and Athletic Trauma
30 East 77th Street, 10th Floor
New York, NY 10021, USA
+1 212 434 2700
www.nismat.org

National Sports Medicine Institute
32 Devonshire Street
London W1G 6PX, UK
+44 (0)20 7908 3636
www.nsmi.org.uk

Sports Massage Association
P.O. Box 44347
London SW19 1WD, UK
+44 (0)20 8545 0861
www.thesma.org

www.physsportsmed.com
Sports medicine online.

EQUIPMENT AND GADGETS

The Baby Jogger Company
P.O. Box 2189
Yakima, WA 98907, USA
+1 509 457 0925
www.babyjogger.com

Leisure Systems International
Northfield Road, Southam,
Warwickshire CV47 0RD, UK
+44 (0)1926 816177
Powerbreathe devices; fitness gadgets and accessories.

Life Fitness
10601 W. Belmont Ave.
Franklin Park, IL 60131, USA
+1 847 288 3300
www.lifefitness.com

NordicTrack
+1 800 220 1256
www.nordictrack.com
Home exercise equipment

www.polar.com or
www.cardiosport.com
Heart-rate monitors.

SPORT AND FITNESS CAMPS

FitCamps
PO Box 473, Richmond
Surrey TW9 4SJ, UK
+44 (0)845 0573135
www.fitcamps.com
Fitness "weekenders" in the UK and Europe.

Jeff Galloway
www.jeffgalloway.com
Running camps across the USA.

Leisure Pursuits Group
Cable House, Hunts Common
Hartley Wintney
Hampshire RG27 8AB, UK
+44 (0)800 0186101
www.lpgleisurepursuits.co.uk
Training camps in Europe and the UK including at sports resorts such as Club la Santa.

Malcolm Balk
balkm@videotron.ca
Running workshops in Canada and Europe.

Sports Tours International
91 Walkden Road, Worsley
Manchester M28 7BQ, UK
+44 (0)161 703 8161
Cycling, running, and triathlon.

TrailPlus
21 Glossop Road
Charlesworth, Glossop
Derbyshire SK13 5HB, UK
+44 (0)1457 855425
www.trailplus.com
Marathon training camps and adventure racing weekends.

ACKNOWLEDGMENTS

All photography by Chris Everard unless otherwise stated. Photographs on page 47: Francesca Yorke (left), Peter Cassidy (center), Nicky Dowey (right).

The publishers would like to thank our models Claire, Neal, Cassandra, Nick, and Jasper the dog. Many thanks also to Holmes Place at Canary Riverside and to Wandsworth Council.

Holmes Place at Canary Riverside, 34 Westferry Circus, Canary Wharf, London E14 8RR, UK
+44 (0)20 7513 2999, www.holmesplace.com

First published in 2004
in the United Kingdom by
Ryland Peters & Small
Kirkman House
12–14 Whitfield Street
London W1T 2RP

and in the USA by
Ryland Peters & Small, Inc.
519 Broadway
5th Floor
New York, NY 10012
www.rylandpeters.com

Text, design, and photographs
© Ryland Peters & Small 2004
10 9 8 7 6 5 4 3 2 1

ISBN 1 84172 628 1

All rights reserved. No part of this publication may be reproduced, stored in a retrieval system, or transmitted in any form or by any means, electronic, mechanical, photocopying, or otherwise, without the prior permission of the publisher.

Senior designer Catherine Griffin
Senior editor Henrietta Heald
Picture research Claire Hector
Production Deborah Wehner
Art director Gabriella Le Grazie
Publishing director Alison Starling

Printed and bound in China.

Editorial consultant Christina Rodenbeck

Note: While the advice and information in this journal are believed to be correct at the time of going to press, the author and publisher can accept no legal responsibility or liability for any errors or omissions that may be made. This journal is not designed to be a comprehensive reference book on fitness and the reader should always consult a physician in all matters relating to health and particularly in respect of any symptoms which may require diagnosis or medical attention.